7/89

£2.50

BANGOR CATHEDRAL

Photograph by Geoffrey Charles

The Central Tower from the South-East, showing the Norman Buttress

HISTORY OF BANGOR DIOCESE
(*General Editor*: A. H. DODD)

VOLUME I

BANGOR CATHEDRAL

by

M. L. CLARKE

CARDIFF
UNIVERSITY OF WALES PRESS
1969

PRINTED IN WALES
BY D. BROWN AND SONS, LTD.,
EASTGATE PRESS, COWBRIDGE, GLAM.
(E8383)

FOREWORD

This volume inaugurates what it is hoped will become a standard history of the diocese of Bangor. It is now not far from a century since the late Archdeacon D. R. Thomas produced, single-handed, the first edition of his history of the sister diocese of St. Asaph, and well over half a century since the definitive three-volume edition appeared. The St. Deiniol Historical Society undertook a few years ago to sponsor a similar work for Bangor, but the diocese could not provide another Archdeacon Thomas, and the work was distributed among a team of contributors with an editorial committee to determine policy and myself as general editor.

It was felt that the history of the cathedral called for separate treatment in a volume which should serve as an introduction to the whole series, and the committee counts itself most fortunate to have enlisted for this task the deep and abiding interest in church architecture of Professor M. L. Clarke, Professor of Latin in the University College of North Wales.

Volume II will consist of a chronological history of the diocese for the earliest times to the present day. It is planned, subject to such modifications as may prove necessary, as follows:

Chapter I (Earliest times to 1120): Rev. Chancellor J. W. James, D.D.

,, II (1120-1536): Idris Foster, M.A. (Professor of Celtic in the University of Oxford)

,, III (1536-1662): A. H. Dodd, M.A., Hon.D.Litt. (Professor Emeritus of History in the University of Wales)

,, IV (1662-1735): Ven. Archdeacon E. G. Wright, M.A., B.D.

,, V (1735-1811)

,, VI (1811-1859): W. Ogwen Williams, M.A. (Professor of Welsh History, University College of Wales, Aberystwyth)

,, VII (1860-1920): Very Rev. Gwynfryn Richards, M.A., B.Sc. (Dean of Bangor)

Chapter VIII (from 1920): C. L. Mowat, M.A., Ph.D. (Professor of History, University College of North Wales, Bangor)

The work will be completed in two further volumes containing brief histories of the parishes, grouped in their rural deaneries. Each volume will be illustrated.

The work is being produced by the University of Wales Press in conjunction with the St. Deiniol Historical Society. To make possible the completion of what will inevitably be a costly enterprise, the Society looks forward with confidence to generous financial support from public bodies interested in the history of the district and of its religious life and institutions.

A. H. DODD
Hon. Editor

CONTENTS

LIST OF ILLUSTRATIONS

The Author and the University of Wales Press Board wish to acknowledge with gratitude the help given by the Dean of Bangor, the Very Reverend Gwynfryn Richards in providing the illustrations.

ABBREVIATIONS

Arch. Camb.	*Archaeologia Cambrensis*
Browne Willis	Browne Willis, *Survey of the Cathedral Church of Bangor*, 1721.
C.P.L.	*Calendar of Papal Registers, Papal Letters*
C.P.P.	*Calendar of Papal Petitions*
C.P.R.	*Calendar of Patent Rolls*
C.S.P.	*Calendar of State Papers*
C.A.	Chapter Acts (N.L.W., B/DC/V, 1-5.)
Hughes, *Cotton*	William Hughes, *Life and Speeches of the Very Reverend J. H. Cotton*, 1874.
Hughes, *Recollections*	William Hughes, *Recollections of Bangor Cathedral*, 1904.
N.L.W.	National Library of Wales.
N.W.C.	*North Wales Chronicle*
N.W.G.	*North Wales Gazette*
P.P.	Parliamentary Papers
Pring	Joseph Pring, *Papers, Documents, Law Proceedings, etc., etc., respecting the Maintenance of the Choir of the Cathedral Church of Bangor*, 1819.
R.C.A.M.	Royal Commission on Ancient Monuments in Wales and Monmouthshire.
Storer	J. S. Storer, *History and Antiquities of the Cathedrals of Great Britain*, 1814-1818, vol. I
T.A.A.S.	*Transactions of the Anglesey Antiquarian Society*
Visitations	A transcript of answers to visitations of 1560, 1567, 1617, 1620, 1623 and 1632 now in U.C.N.W. Library. (Those of 1617 to 1632 are also to be found in N.L.W., B/QA/1) Reference is given to the respondent and the year of the visitation.

CHAPTER I

THE CATHEDRAL STRUCTURE AND FITTINGS

(i) PRE-REFORMATION

The architectural history of Bangor cathedral begins in the twelfth century.[1] Of the buildings that existed before then we know nothing. Analogy with early monastic sites in Ireland suggests that the original settlement consisted of a number of small buildings without any regular plan, and it has been supposed that the foundations discovered in College Park in 1925 were part of such a settlement; but excavations undertaken in 1964 failed to reveal any traces of buildings elsewhere in the Park, and it seems more likely that the site of the present cathedral was also that of the monastery founded by St. Deiniol in the sixth century. This monastery was sacked in 634 and again in 1073,[2] and the church built by Deiniol had no doubt been rebuilt by the twelfth century. The first church was probably of wood, but this may well have been replaced by one of stone; in default of other evidence we may imagine something like the church at Llandaff which Bishop Urban found on his appointment to the see in 1107, twenty-eight feet long, fifteen feet wide and twenty feet high, with very small transeptal annexes and an apsidal chancel twelve feet long and of the same width.[3]

The building of the Norman church can be ascribed with a fair degree of certainty to the episcopate of David (1120-39),[4] and to the efforts of Gruffydd ap Cynan, who was responsible for the appointment of David, and who gave money to the

---

[1] The best architectural history of the cathedral is that in R.C.A.M. Caerns Inventory II, pp. 1-9. I am also indebted to Harold Hughes's articles in *Arch. Camb.* 1901, pp. 179-204; 1902, pp. 261-6; 1904, pp. 17-32 (abbreviated version in *Old Churches of Snowdonia*, pp. 166-96.) Miss Enid Pierce Roberts has kindly helped me with the Welsh sources for the history of the cathedral, and the Dean of Bangor, the Very Reverend Gwynfryn Richards, has provided information on work done in recent years.

[2] J. E. Lloyd, *History of Wales*, p. 193; *Transactions of the Cymmrodorion Society* 1899-1900, p. 172.

[3] *Liber Landavensis* (ed. W. J. Rees, 1840), p. 82.

[4] For the arguments for David rather than Hervé see *Arch. Camb.* 1949, p 258.

cathedral and was buried in it by the high altar.[5] It was a cruciform building some 130 feet in length. The crossing arches stood in the same position as the present arches; there was an apsidal choir, and the nave extended to the level of the second pier from the west of the present arcade. The south transept, twelve feet shorter than the existing one, had an eastern apse, and a similar plan may be assumed for the north transept.[6] Whether the nave was aisled is not known, but the dimensions of the church as otherwise established suggest that it was not. Of this Norman church the only visible remnant is a part of the south wall of the choir; here can be seen a blocked round-headed window and a flat buttress, the setting of which shows that the spring of the apse was at this point.

In the thirteenth century the Norman apse was removed and the choir extended to its present length; parts of two lancet windows dating from this period can still be seen on the inside of the south wall, on either side of the large perpendicular window. Towards the end of the century a beginning was made with the rebuilding and enlargement of the transepts. The church had suffered in the wars of Edward I, and in 1284 the Dean and Chapter received £60 compensation for damages sustained.[7] Even apart from this evidence it is natural to associate the rebuilding with the end of the wars and with the episcopate of the first Bishop Anian (1267-1307), who was regarded with favour by King Edward. Though the rebuilding of the transepts and crossing was part of a single scheme, it took some time to complete. The south transept was rebuilt first, the north later, the completion of the work being probably due to the second Anian (Anian Sais), bishop from 1309 to 1328. The present transepts and crossing are in the main the work of Scott, but when he undertook his restoration sufficient remnants survived of the work of the late thirteenth to early fourteenth centuries to enable him to reconstruct this part of the church as

---

[5] *History of Gruffydd ap Cynan* (ed. Arthur Jones), pp. 154-6.

[6] The plan of the crossing, choir and south transept was established by Scott, the site of the west end by Henry Barber in 1873; the apse of the south transept was excavated in 1946. (*Arch. Camb.* 1949, pp. 256-61).

[7] *Littere Wallie*, ed. J. Goronwy Edwards, 1940, No. 180, p. 90. In the same year Bishop Anian was paid £250 compensation *pro dampnis nobis illatis in ultima guerra*, a phrase which suggests that this damage was to episcopal property rather than to the cathedral. (*ibid.*, No. 179.)

it then was. The original crossing arches were undoubtedly a good deal lower than the present ones,[8] but the transepts appear to have been faithfully restored.

An arch in the east wall of the south transept led to a chapel, which replaced the old Norman apse; it extended some twenty-two feet to the east, and had an annexe, probably used as a sacristy, on the south side.[9] In the wall between the choir and the chapel was an arched tomb, which still survives though now hidden by stalls and covered by a wall on the outside. There was a similar arrangement on the north side. There too an arch in the east wall of the transept led to a chapel, and there was an arched tomb between the chapel and the choir.[10] It seems highly likely that this was the tomb of Anian II, who was buried in the cathedral in 1328 "in a certain wall" (*in quodam muro*) between the choir and the altar.[11] If the stalls were then under the crossing arches, a position just to the east of these fits in with the recorded site of the tomb, and if the second Anian was responsible for the work on the north transept it would be natural for him to be buried on this side. Similarly if Anian I built the south transept it is a reasonable assumption that the tomb still surviving on the south side is his.

The chapel on the north appears to have extended to the level of the east end of the choir. This part of the cathedral was much altered in the eighteenth century and completely rebuilt by Scott, and its history is not easy to reconstruct, but Scott built on the old ground plan and assigned the base of the previously existing walls to the same date as the north transept.[12] The discovery during his restoration of the fourteenth-century "Eva slab" in the floor by the north wall of this building near its east end confirms the dating and suggests that it was originally

---

[8] This is clear from Storer's engraving (Plate 1), done before the removal of the original arches in 1824.

[9] *Arch. Camb.*, 1949, p. 260.

[10] The tomb was discovered by Scott. See his *Second Report* (1870), p. 28, and J. O. Scott's plan in *The Builder* CXIII (1892) between pages 186 and 187. It was removed by Scott to give place to the arch leading to the organ chamber.

[11] Browne Willis, p. 74.

[12] Scott, *Second Report* (1870), p. 16; J. O. Scott's plan in *The Builder* (see Note 10). Browne Willis's statement that the structure was enlarged in the eighteenth century, "the old foundation not being near so capacious as the present" seems to be erroneous. Browne Willis, p. 310, cf. p. 321.

a chapel.[13] It has been identified with the chapel of the two Saints John, the Baptist and the Evangelist, to which Bishop Cliderow bequeathed two altar coverings in 1435;[14] but the size of the structure makes it far more probable that it was the Lady Chapel, in which case the smaller chapel on the south would be that of the Saints John.

Whether a central tower was built at this period is uncertain. The Norman church almost certainly had one, and this may have been the scene of the betrayal of Llywelyn ap Gruffydd recorded as having taken place in 1282 "in the belfry at Bangor."[15] A belfry is said to have been burnt in 1309,[16] a date which could be either prior or subsequent to the rebuilding of the crossing. It is clear however that there was no tower after the reconstruction of the church *c.* 1500, though the crossing arches survived, and one would expect the collapse or removal of a central tower to have been accompanied by that of the arches on which it stood. It is possible that the Norman tower was never rebuilt and that the belfry referred to in the documents stood elsewhere. But a central tower was no doubt intended, even if it was not built, and the spiral staircase in the north-east corner of the north transept, which no doubt dates in part at any rate from the early fourteenth century rebuilding, was presumably designed to provide access to a tower.

The history of the nave after the building of the Norman church is obscure. In 1873 excavations revealed the foundation of a wall partly under the existing south wall, but projecting two feet eight inches into the church.[17] No dressed stone was found to give an indication of date. As the wall was traced as far as the present south door, beyond the west end of the original Norman church, it cannot belong to an aisle of that church, and

---

13 The slab was surrounded by fourteenth-century tiles and had a later tiled floor above it. Hughes and North, *Old Churches of Snowdonia*, pp. 189-90. For its original postion see *The Builder*, 1892, p. 187. It is now at the west end of the north aisle. In Browne Willis's day a wall of 2 ft. 6 ins. separated the westernmost room (storeroom) from the middle one (vestry), but the vestry was separated from the chapter room to the east only by a 6 ins. partition (Browne Willis, p. 20). This might possibly indicate two periods of building, but the evidence of fourteenth-century work in the eastern part shows that they cannot have been far apart.

14 Browne Willis, pp. 88-9, 232.

15 *Brut y Twysogyon* (Peniarth MS) ed. Thomas Jones, 1952, p. 120.

16 R.C.A.M., quoting P.R.O., Ancient Petitions E 769.

17 The excavation was made by Henry Barber, and is recorded by Harold Hughes in *Arch. Camb.* 1901, p. 188.

as it bears no relation to the arch between the south transept and the present aisle, it must be earlier than the rebuilding of the transept. We are forced to assume that at some unknown date between the building of the Norman church and the end of the thirteenth century the nave was extended and a south aisle added.[18]

The arches leading from the transepts to the aisles, which were, so far as can be judged, correctly reconstructed by Scott, imply either the existence of aisles of the present width or the intention to build them. The present aisles were not built until well after the transepts, and there is no evidence of the previous existence of aisles apart from the mysterious foundation already mentioned. If a wall on this foundation existed when the south transept was rebuilt, the arch leading from the transept would have cut into it; if there was no north aisle when the north transept was rebuilt, the corresponding arch on that side would have led nowhere. Perhaps these arches were blocked up until the aisles which had evidently been projected were eventually completed.

The dating of the fourteenth-century rebuilding of the nave presents some difficulties. On stylistic grounds one would be inclined to assign the aisle windows to the early part of the century, but documentary evidence which deserves respect points to a later date. In 1386 the bishop, John Swaffham, stated in a petition that for twenty-six years and more Bangor had been without a church, and that he had begun one which was now half constructed; he was unable to complete the work because of the meagreness of his revenues and because of certain payments due to the king which he asked to have remitted.[19] The "church" to which he referred was evidently the nave of the cathedral, and his petition, if it is to be taken literally, shows that the old nave was taken down in or before 1360, during the episcopate of Bishop Ringstede,[20] and that

[18] Excavations in 1873 also revealed rubble masonry, apparently the foundation of piers, on the line of the south arcade to the west of each of the first two existing piers. (See Henry Barber's plan in N.L.W., B/Maps 24). These foundations do not appear to be in the right place for the fourteenth-century piers, and presumably are connected with the extension of the nave referred to above.

[19] *C.P.R.* 1385-9, p. 187. In the same year Swaffham obtained for the cathedral the benefices of Llanynys and Llanfair Dyffryn Clwyd to maintain four chaplains and for the repair of the church. *ibid.*, pp. 189-90.

[20] Ringstede left £100 for the restoration of the cathedral. The legacy was on condition that his successor was an Englishman; if he was not, the matter was left to the discretion of his executors. (Browne Willis, p. 217). As the next bishop was a Welshman the legacy may not have been put into effect.

rebuilding did not begin until Swaffham became bishop in 1376 and was only half finished ten years later. As the petition was successful we may assume that the work was completed soon after 1386. The poem of Dafydd ap Gwilym addressed to the Dean, Hywel ap Gronow, and therefore dating from before 1370, unfortunately does not tell us more than that the cathedral was then in use; the "whitewashed church was its fine organ" (tŷ geirwgalch teg ei organ) of which he writes could have consisted of choir and transepts only.[21]

Of the rebuilding of the nave the aisle walls survive. The arcades have been replaced, but the western respond of the south one can still be seen in the projecting wall with which the present arcade terminates. Its position shows that the fourteenth-century arcades, unlike the present ones, were of seven bays and corresponded with the aisle windows. They were on a line slightly different from that of the existing arcades. During Scott's restoration the base of the eastern respond of the south arcade was found projecting eighteen inches into the south aisle and at the west end of the north arcade traces can still be seen of a base projecting the same distance into the north aisle. No evidence has been discovered of a respond in the south-east corner of the north aisle, but it is a reasonable assumption that the north arcade was throughout its length slightly to the north of the present arcade and parallel to the outer wall, as the south arcade was (more or less) parallel to the south aisle wall. When the arcades were rebuilt in the early sixteenth century an error was made in siting that on the south. At the east it was slightly to the north of the old line, but it joined that line at the west, and is therefore not parallel with the outer wall but closer to it at the west than at the east.[22]

In 1402, so tradition has it, the cathedral was burnt to the ground in Owain Glyndŵr's rising. The tradition goes back to the time of Elizabeth I, when Camden in his *Britannia* described the cathedral as having been burnt by "that most profligate rebel

---

[21] *Gwaith Dafydd ap Gwilym*, ed. T. Parry, 1952, p. 42.

[22] For a different view see R.C.A.M., where it is stated that the fourteenth-century arcades did not run parallel to the north and south walls and that this was corrected in the sixteenth-century rebuilding. Whatever may be the case with regard to the north arcade, on the south the fourteenth-century arcade appears to have been more nearly parallel to the outer wall than is the present arcade.

Owen Glyn Dowrdwy",[23] but there seems to be no contemporary evidence of this destruction. If damage was done, as is likely enough in view of the devastation recorded elsewhere in Wales, it did not involve the whole of the cathedral, for in 1409 Bishop Nicholls was enthroned "with due and customary solemnity and ceremony."[24] A new font was acquired in the early fifteenth century, and if this was in the customary place near the main entrance, the nave must then have been in a fit state for the administering of baptism.[25] The eastern parts of the cathedral were evidently in use in 1435, since Bishop Cliderow in his will of that year directed that if he died in or near Bangor he was to be buried in the chapel of Saints John, and left various vestments and altar coverings to the cathedral.[26] The agreement made with the Vicars in 1445 by which they undertook the conduct of the cathedral services is further evidence of the continued use of the building.[27]

Cliderow's will directed that the church should be covered with shingles, and if this was carried into effect the building should have been put in a sound state; but in 1469 we find Bishop Ednam in a petition for permission to hold a benefice *in commendam* complaining that he was unable to repair the church although it was threatened with ruin.[28] His petition was successful, but there is no evidence of his having repaired the cathedral, and it seems that by the fifteen-twenties the nave had been roofless for some time. This at any rate is implied by the poet Dafydd Trefor, who writing in praise of Bishop Skevington's rebuilding of the nave speaks of it as having been previously grassgrown (tir glas fu).[29]

---

23 Camden, *Britannia*, English Translation 1695, col. 665. The sentence in its Latin form is in the first edition (1586), pp. 387-8.

24 *Arch. Camb.* 1922, p. 86. It is interesting to find this point made in a letter from Owen Lloyd to Browne Willis of 1719. (Bodleian MS Jesus College 115, p. 404). Willis however ignored the evidence of Nicholls's enthronement in his *Survey*.

25 Before 1824 the font was against the third pier from the west on the south side, but as it dates from before the existing arcades, this may not have been its original position.

26 Browne Willis, pp. 231-2.

27 See pp. 52-3.

28 *C.P.L.* XII, p. 668. Bishop Stanbury, who died in 1474, some years after his translation from Bangor, left £30 to the cathedral fabric. Browne Willis, p. 91.

29 *T.A.A.S.*, 1935, p. 99.

Towards the end of the fifteenth century an extensive reconstruction was begun which was completed in 1532. According to a tradition which goes back to the sixteenth century the first stage of the work was undertaken by Henry Deane, bishop from 1494 to 1500.[30] But a poem by Guto'r Glyn addressed to Richard Kyffin, dean from 1480 to 1502, describes him as reroofing the choir,[31] and as the writer is believed to have died about 1493 it appears that this was done before Deane's appointment. The work however probably went on into Deane's episcopate, and he is said to have left his crozier and mitre to his successor on condition that he would finish the work he had begun.[32] In addition to the reroofing of the choir new windows were inserted. The east window, which differs stylistically from the others, may be earlier in date; the large one on the south and the smaller ones on the same side at a higher level were evidently completed during Kyffin's decanate. One of the smaller windows contained glass with the inscription *Orate pro bono statu Ricardi Kyffin*,[33] a formula which implies that he was alive at the time the glass was inserted. We can therefore with some confidence assign the completion of the choir to before 1502.

Work was also done on the transepts. The south chapel, which was perhaps already in ruins, was removed, and some of its masonry was reused in the transept;[34] at the same time a large five-light window was made in the south wall of the transept. A similar window was inserted in the north transept, and both transepts were finished off, as was the choir, with low-pitched roofs and battlements.

What happened to the Lady Chapel on the north is not clear. The blocked openings on the north of the choir ought to provide some indication of the history of this part of the building, but they are not easy to interpret. If the opening to the east of the organ chamber belongs to a former window (and it is hard to see what else it could have been), it would seem that when it was inserted the chapel, or part of it, had been removed. The

---

30 Camden's *Britannia* (1586), pp. 387-8.

31 *Gwaith Guto'r Glyn* (ed. Ifor Williams, 1939), p. 247.

32 Browne Willis, p. 95. Miss Pierce Roberts informs me that a poem perhaps by Elis ap Siôn ap Morys (Peniarth MSS 71, pp. 73-9) written in praise of Deane does not mention any work of his on the cathedral.

33 Browne Willis, pp. 17-18.

34 *Arch. Camb.* 1949, pp. 260-61.

adjacent blocked doorway seems to indicate a change in the arrangements on this side of the choir. Perhaps it led to a chapter house or vestry newly constructed on the old foundations; and this reconstruction must have necessitated the blocking of the window, the bottom of which is on a level with the top of the doorway. It was perhaps at this period too that the arches between the transepts and the aisles were walled up. As Browne Willis's plan shows, in the early eighteenth century there were only narrow openings between aisles and transepts, and the fact that Scott when he reconstructed the arches found only parts of them *in situ* suggests that they disappeared in the course of a radical reconstruction such as was undertaken at this period.

The removal of the south chapel and the probable alterations on the north side of the choir must have involved simultaneous work on both choir and transepts; and the fact that Kyffin was buried in the south transept suggests that it was completed before his death. It therefore seems likely that the reconstruction of both choir and transepts belonged to the first stage of the work, and was completed by about 1500, before the nave was rebuilt.[35]

Work on the nave was undertaken by Bishop Skevington, who, as stated in the inscription over the tower doorway, built the tower and the church (*hoc campaniele et ecclesiam fieri fecit*) in 1532. The phrase *ecclesiam fieri fecit* refers to the new arcade and clerestorey inserted within the fourteenth-century outer walls. This work was evidently completed before the tower was built, since Dafydd Trefor gives the date at which Skevington "put the top on the wall" as 1527.[36] Though the arcades and the tower were part of the same scheme, it is a curious fact that they are not exactly related to one another, since the tower arch is nearer to the north than to the south arcade. This has been explained on the supposition that the tower was planned in relation to the fourteenth-century arches, which, as we have seen, were on a different line, and that the present arch is in the position of a previous fourteenth-century arch designed to lead into a tower.[37] A simpler explanation would be that Skevington's

[35] For a different view see R.A.C.M., Caerns Inventory II, p. 3.
[36] *T.A.A.S.*, 1935, p. 100. The date is wrongly given by R.C.A.M. as 1525.
[37] R.C.A.M., Caerns Inventory II, p. 6.

architect intended to place the tower centrally in relation not to the arcades but to the width of nave and aisles combined.[38] The fact that at the west end the south aisle is narrower than the north makes it appear from the inside that the tower is further to the north than it in fact is.

The tower was not completed when Skevington died in 1533. In his will he directed that "the Steeple and Lofte of Bangor churche where the Bells doo hange be fynished, and the three Bells hanged up, and a further Belle agreeable to them be providid and hangid there, and that the roofe of that Steple to be well made, coverid with Leade, and the Windowe in the said Steple over the Doore to be well Barride with Yron and glased."[39] There is a tradition that the tower was designed to be carried up higher, but that Skevington's executors "immediately covered it up and so left it".[40] Such a story could easily have arisen to explain the unimpressive character of the belfry stage; Skevington's will suggests that the tower was finished in all essentials at the time of his death.

One would not have expected the reign of Henry VIII to be a period when much was done to the cathedral fabric. Yet in addition to the extensive work of Skevington, Arthur Bulkeley, bishop from 1541 to 1553, spent £42 on "the Roofe and Leads of the South Side of the Church, which before was ready to fall,"[41] and a number of bequests, though in some cases only small ones, were made for the repair and adornment of the building in the fifteen-twenties and fifteen-thirties.[42] No doubt some pressure was put on testators to remember the cathedral in their wills. One of Bishop Bulkeley's injunctions of 1542 was that the clergy when called in to draw up wills should "diligently procure excite and stirre and exhorte" the testators to make a bequest to the cathedral fabric.[43]

Let us now try to picture the interior of the cathedral as it was on the eve of the Reformation. The windows of the choir and transepts were filled with recently installed stained glass, which

[38] He did not succeed in doing so; but this is not an argument in favour of the R.C.A.M. theory, since the tower is no more exactly central to the fourteenth-century nave than to the total width of the church.

[39] Browne Willis, p. 246.

[40] *ibid.*, p. 23.

[41] Browne Willis, p. 258.

[42] *Arch. Camb.* 1878, pp. 148-61.

[43] Bodleian MS Jesus College 115, pp. 379-86.

survived, though in a fragmentary state, until the eighteenth century. On the north wall near the high altar was the picture of St. Deiniol before which Bishop Skevington's heart was buried.[44] The flooring of the choir would, in part at any rate, be of ornamental tiles, some of which Scott discovered in the course of his restoration and copied in the present flooring; but much of the floor must have been composed of the tombstones of the clerics buried in the vicinity of the altar. The stalls, as is indicated by the level of the four small windows, were to the east of the choir arch; under the arch would be a screen, and on it probably the organ, mentioned by Dafydd Trefor in the poem referred to above. In the transepts would be altars. If we are right in supposing that the old Lady Chapel had been put to other uses, the north transept would have taken its place, and it is interesting to find Richard Motton, a vicar of the cathedral, leaving twenty shillings in 1536 towards "the making of a vaute over the lady-aulter",[45] which in view of the small sum bequeathed can hardly have been more than a projecting canopy or tester. The south transept would also have its altar, perhaps still dedicated to the two Saints John, unless it had been appropriated to the chantry of St. Catherine, founded by Dean Kyffin, the altar of which may be assumed to have been in this transept as it was here that he was buried.[46] Somewhere else in the cathedral was an altar of St. Michael at which another chantry priest, on Maurice Glynn's foundation, officiated.[47] The nave, though recently rebuilt, must have been somewhat cheerless. The floor was of earth, and, as is evident from the different levels of the north and south doorways and by the fact that the piers of the north arcade are higher from base to cap than those of the south, no attempt had been made to correct the slope

[44] *Arch. Camb.* 1876, p. 223. Browne Willis (pp. 17, 98) supposed the reference to be to a representation of St. Deiniol still visible in his day in one of the small windows on the south of the choir. But according to Humphrey Humphreys in Wood, *Athenae Oxonienses* II, col. 742, Skevington's heart was buried in a small lead coffin by the north wall within the altar rails. It was covered by a loose flagstone which the schoolboys used to remove in order to take out the coffin. After Humphreys had gone to Oxford one of the boys opened the coffin "and the heart was very entire; but upon the letting in the air, it begun to turn to dust." After this the coffin was soldered up and buried securely. There was no trace of the picture of St. Deiniol in Humphreys's day.

[45] *Arch. Camb.* 1878, p. 151.

[46] Browne Willis, p. 34.

[47] See copy of the foundation deed in Bodleian MS Jesus College 115, p. 367.

of the ground from south to north.[48] Skevington's work was not in itself of very high quality, and it is unlikely that much was done to adorn the interior before the reformers began to wage war on "superstitious images".

(ii) POST-REFORMATION

The cathedral as we know it today is a mixture of pre-Reformation and Victorian work. The successive restorations of the nineteenth century removed all traces of work done in the intervening period, and a modern visitor might be tempted to suppose that nothing was done between Bishop Skevington and Gilbert Scott. This is by no means the case. Throughout this period the structure was kept in repair, and was fitted and adorned in accordance with the needs and the taste of the day.

In the early seventeenth century the nave and transept roofs were ceiled. This was, in part at any rate, financed by contributions from the clergy of the diocese, who had been summoned by Bishop Rowlands to a convocation in the cathedral. A letter of his of 1611 calls upon nine curates to send their contributions of 6/8d. each on pain of excommunication, refers to the "lamentable ruin" of the building and states that carpenters are already at work.[49] The work then done was still to be seen in 1721, when Browne Willis wrote of the nave ceiling of nine beams "well wrought and beautify'd with carved work", with four panels between each beam. The date 1611 was to be seen on the roofs of nave and transepts, and in the transepts the name of Bishop Rowlands, whose coat of arms, with that of his predecessor Richard Vaughan (1595-7) was on the nave ceiling. Under Rowlands's successor Lewis Bayly releading was found necessary, especially of the choir roof and of the western part of the nave roof. Appealing for help to Sir John Wynn in 1626 Bayly wrote that the cathedral "this rainy weather for want of a better mantle, weepeth, that it makes my heart bleed to see her".[50]

[48] Steps down from the south door and down to the north were put in when the floor was paved. Paving involved covering the lower part of the plinths of the north arcade.

[49] N.L.W., B/Misc. Vols. /23, p. 71. The same method was used to raise money for the fabric in 1561, though no work is otherwise recorded as having been done then. *Ibid.* pp. 214-7.

[50] Calendar of Wynn Papers, No. 1440. Cf. 1445 where he refers to repairing the windows. Rowlands had left a legacy of £20 towards releading. Pring, p. 146.

The sentiments, if not the words, must have been those of many of the cathedral clergy before and after. It appears that Bayly's appeals had little success, for in 1630 he claimed to have spent £600 out of his own purse on the repair of the cathedral.[51]

During the Commonwealth the Prayer Book services were forbidden and the organ was presumably destroyed or removed in accordance with the Parliamentary Order of 1644 "for the speedy demolishing of all organs, images and all matters of superstitious monuments in all cathedrals . . . throughout the kingdom of England and the Dominion of Wales."[52] With the restoration of the king came the restoration of the church services, and the Chapter set about refitting the cathedral. Stalls and choir seats, a canopied bishop's throne and an organ were installed, the organ being paid for from a legacy of £100 left by Bishop William Roberts, who died in 1665, and erected by his successor Robert Morgan.[53] On the organ case was a Latin verse inscription, in which the two bishops who had provided the money and erected the organ were compared to David and Solomon respectively.

Materiam Templi Rex David praebuit olim,
Sed Solomon sanctam condidit ipse Domum.
Sic sumptum ut David Gulielmus praebuit amplum,
Robertus struxit sacrum opus ut Solomon.[54]

Which might be translated:

As Solomon of old did cause to rise
The sacred temple by King David planned,
So was achieved this holy enterprise
By William's bounty and by Robert's hand.

In 1697 a sum of £50 left by Edward Wynne, Chancellor of the cathedral, was used to put up panelling round the east end, with fluted pilasters on either side of the altar.[55]

The organ was on a screen under the eastern crossing arch, with the stalls for clergy and choir to the east of it. Here the

---

[51] *Trans. Cymmrodorion Soc.* 1928-9, p. 122.

[52] P. A. Scholes, *The Puritans and Music,* p. 232.

[53] Browne Willis, p. 16. Roberts's executors gave an extra £80. *Arch. Camb.*, 1925, p. 46.

[54] Browne Willis, p. 16.

[55] *Ibid.* p. 11. C.A., May 28, 1697. Wynne had died in 1669. The sum he bequeathed was "recovered by Bishop Humphreys out of desperate hands," Browne Willis p. 162.

English services were performed; the parochial part of the building was in the area to the west of the organ screen, in the transepts and crossing space, where the Welsh congregation was accommodated, the men sitting in the south transept, the women in the north. The nave was bare and unused; in the early eighteenth century it was partly paved, but the aisles and the west part of the nave still had earthen floors and were used for burials.[56] The west end of the north aisle was fitted up as the Consistory Court, and the tower arch was filled with a screen. This was a mixture of classic and Gothic work, the latter perhaps re-used from the pre-reformation screen.[57]

During the episcopate of Humphrey Lloyd steps were taken to obtain an endowment for the cathedral. Hitherto, as Browne Willis puts it, the cathedral services and fabric were "supported solely by Contributions of the Bishop and Chapter; and what they would get by begging from other Persons in the Diocese was apply'd to the same use."[58] Although the building served as parish church as well as cathedral, the parishioners did not contribute to its expenses. An attempt was made in 1637 to make them do so through a church rate; some of those assessed refused to pay and were excommunicated, whereupon they sent in a petition to Archbishop Laud,[59] and apparently got their way, since in 1684 it was stated that the parishioners made no contribution to the upkeep of the cathedral.[60] The bishop's plan was to appropriate to the cathedral the comportionary rectory of Llandinam in Montgomeryshire, comprising the parishes of Llandinam, Llanidloes, Trefeglwys, Llanwnog and Carno, which had previously been held as a sinecure by absentee clerics.[61] The scheme approved by Parliament in 1685 was that one-third of the benefice should go to the vicars of Llandinam and two-thirds to the cathedral, "for the Repair and Support of the Fabrick . . . and for the Maintenance of the Choir."[62] According to the preamble of the Act of Parliament the cathedral was "very ruinous". The term "ruinous" then meant rather less

[56] *Ibid.*, pp. 19, 2, 10.
[57] See Storer, plate 2.
[58] Browne Willis, p. 30.
[59] *C.S.P. Dom.* 1636-7, p. 375.
[60] *Arch. Camb.* 1925, p. 60.
[61] For the background of the 1685 Act see *Arch. Camb.* 1925, pp. 45-73.
[62] Browne Willis, p. 293.

than it now does, and there were those at the time who doubted whether the needs of the fabric were as great as was represented;[63] but old buildings constantly need repair, and it was undeniably useful for the Cathedral to possess this endowment. In 1722 Dean John Jones could report in reply to Visitation questions that the building was "in better repair than it hath bin these many years", though he added that much remained to be done.[64]

The roofs continued to require attention. In 1717 the relatively large sum of £127 11s. 9½d. was paid to a plumber, presumably for work on the roof. In 1741 the roof of the choir was inspected by Rice Jones, carpenter, and William Peters, plumber, who reported that the roof and leads should be renewed as soon as possible.[65] Peters did some work in 1744, and in 1747 another plumber, John Rathbone, was paid £60 for releading the choir.[66] Other references to plumbing work occur in the accounts in the following years; but the main work of releading was done in the 1790's. In 1786 John Cooper of Beaumaris was asked to survey the roof of the south aisle and make an estimate for reroofing, and in the next year it was decided that after this work was completed the roofs of the north aisle and nave should be put into repair.[67] The work was begun in 1788 by the plumber Thomas Rathbone and completed in 1790-92 by another plumber, Robert Barnes. The lead pipes which still exist on each side of the nave leading from the main roof to the aisle roofs date from this period, as is shown by the date 1791 on the centre one on each side.[68] The accounts for 1791 show a payment of £152 17s. 6d. for timber, which we may assume was for use on the nave roof, and it was probably at this time that most of the work of Bishop Rowlands was removed; the old framework was retained, but the carved ornaments and what Storer calls "historical allusions", meaning perhaps the arms of Bishops Vaughan and Rowlands, disappeared.[69]

---

[63] *Arch. Camb.* 1925, pp. 57-8.
[64] N.L.W., B/Misc. Vols./23, p. 27.
[65] C.A., July 31, 1741.
[66] *Ibid.*, Feb. 3, 1746.
[67] *Ibid.* Aug. 1, 1786; Nov. 9, 1787; Sept. 22, 1790.
[68] The date is wrongly given by R.C.A.M. as 1779. In 1951, before the reroofing of the south aisle, I observed the date 1797 scratched on the lead, with the initials WD, TD and TE.
[69] Storer, pp. (k)-(l). The attribution of this work to the episcopate of Cleaver (1800-1806) seems erroneous.

In 1769 one Robert Lloyd was asked to draw up an estimate "of what may be necessary to decorate the choir",[70] and in 1772 he was paid three guineas for two journeys to Bangor and for making his plans and estimate.[71] It seems doubtful whether these were ever carried out. In 1771 the Chapter accepted a plan drawn up by John Edmund for restoring the choir and steeple, and payments totalling a little more than £284 were made to him for this work.[72] In 1785 £105 was paid to Cooper of Beaumaris for rebuilding the mason's work of the east window; he appears to have reproduced the original tracery with an accuracy surprising in the eighteenth century.[73]

The only structural addition made in the eighteenth century was to the building to the north of the choir, which was by now divided into store room, vestry and chapter house. In 1705 it was decided to erect a library over these rooms "this year if the church fund extends for that purpose."[74] In 1721 the library had been built, but had not yet been fitted up; in that year however the Chapter decided to spend £40 on completing the work.[75] In 1730, after the cathedral had received a legacy of Dean John Jones's books, it was ordered that "the room above the Chapter House be divided and fitted up" to receive these books.[76] A more ambitious work was decided upon in 1776, when it was resolved that the upper room should be converted into one and fitted up as a library and chapter house, while the chapter house below was to become the registry.[77] These alterations necessitated the rebuilding of the upper storey. "Mr. Wyatt the architect" (presumably the famous James Wyatt, though the phrase could refer to his brother Samuel) was asked to draw up plans and estimates, and in 1778 these were accepted.[78]

---

[70] C.A., Aug. 8, 1769. Cf. Aug. 7, 1770.

[71] *Ibid.*, June 16, 1772.

[72] *Ibid.*, April 23, 1771.

[73] The tracery was no doubt renewed again in Scott's restoration, but Storer's engraving (plate 6) shows that after it had left Cooper's hands it was indistinguishable from a fifteenth-century window.

[74] C.A., May 10, 1705.

[75] Browne Willis, p. 19; C.A., Nov. 22, 1721.

[76] *Ibid.*, Aug. 20, 1730.

[77] *Ibid.*, Aug. 6, 1776. According to the Chapter Order the room "now called the library" was to become the registry. This room was apparently used as a Chapter House, since according to Storer (p. (m)) the Chapter House became the Registry.

[78] C.A., Oct. 15, 1776; Oct. 17, 1778. The work was carried out by John Edmund, to whom payments totalling £586 were made in 1779 and 1791.

The new upper storey had three Gothic windows on the north side and at the east one of five lights under a depressed ogee arch.

Certain minor alterations and improvements were made to the interior in the course of the eighteenth century. In 1701 it was decided to discontinue burials in the middle aisle,[79] and in 1730 the paving of this part of the nave was completed at a cost of £76 17s. 6d. In 1753 it was resolved to pave the south aisle,[80] and the accounts show that sums of money were paid to Ralph Hughes for paving in 1755 and 1756. Hyde Hall, writing in 1809-11, states that both aisles were paved; but there appear to have still been some unpaved parts of the nave when the restoration of 1824 was undertaken.[81] Early in the nineteenth century stained glass was inserted in some of the windows of the nave.[82] In 1707 Edward Jones, joiner, was paid £6 for making a pulpit and bishop's throne for the Welsh services. The pulpit was placed against the west pier of the south transept arch, and the throne against the east pier opposite; both were described by Browne Willis as handsome.[83] The throne was still in existence when Hyde Hall wrote, though it had not been used for some years, and it was removed soon after.[84]

In 1729 a legacy of £100 was received from Dean John Jones and was used for the purchase of an altarpiece. This was evidently not made locally; the bishop (Sherlock) was entrusted with its purchase, and the accounts show a payment of £3 1s. 0d. for its carriage from Chester.[85] One would expect it to have been a handsome object, though to an observer of the early nineteenth century it appeared to have been "designed and executed by a common workman of the country."[86] In 1779 a new organ, the gift of Dean Thomas Lloyd, was installed. It cost three hundred and sixty guineas and was made by

[79] C.A., Oct. 20, 1701.
[80] *Ibid.*, July 11, 1753.
[81] Hyde Hall, *Description of Caernarvonshire*, p. 158; Hughes *Cotton*, p. 23.
[82] Evans, *Beauties of North Wales* (1812), p. 440.
[83] Browne Willis, pp. 7, 19.
[84] Hyde Hall, *op. cit.*, p. 157; the throne is not shown in Storer's plate 1.
[85] C.A., July 23, 1729; Aug. 9, 1730.
[86] Storer, p. (k). According to John Evans (*Tour through part of North Wales in the year* 1798, ed. 1800, p. 226) the choir was "fitted up in a style of neat and simple elegance by the munificence of the present prelate" (i.e., Warren). This work must have been of limited scope. It is clear from Storer that the choir fittings in general remained as they were in Browne Willis's time.

Samuel Green, the leading organ builder of the day.[87] At the same time a new organ screen and loft was built by Cooper of Beaumaris.[88] It projected into the crossing space and was supported on two wooden pillars and approached, as the previous loft had been, by a staircase in the north transept. In 1801 the pillars were painted in imitation of stone and the front of the loft in imitation of oak.[89] Storer's view shows a front of feeble Gothic design, which his letterpress describes as a "puerile and mean imitation of the English style of design, as occasionally displayed, with such captivating touches of genius, in the screen work of ancient sacred edifices."[90]

"From the ruinous magnificence of St. David's the examiner turns, with pleasure, to the well preserved fabric of our unaspiring cathedral." So wrote the anonymous author of the description of Bangor in Storer's *Cathedrals*.[91] But the state of the fabric did not justify any complacency. Indeed it is described elsewhere as being " in a deplorable state of dilapidation," with the roof letting in the rain,[92] and according to a survey made in 1816 the battlements of the tower and transepts needed repair, the choir walls were cracking and the western crossing arch was in a dangerous state.[93] Moreover additional accommodation was badly needed. The population of Bangor was increasing rapidly; from 1770 at the first census in 1801 it rose to 3579 twenty years later. The English congregation, which must have been very small for most of the eighteenth century, was reckoned at from 350 to 400 in 1816, whereas the choir where the English services were performed could accommodate at the most 130,[94] and this figure must be that of its potential rather than its actual capacity, since as then arranged it cannot have held many more than the clergy and singing men and boys.[95]

---

87 C.A., Oct. 13, 1778; Sept. 20, 1779.

88 *Ibid.*, Oct. 14, 1780.

89 *Ibid.*, Sept. 28, 1801.

90 Storer, plate 1 and p. (l).

91 *Ibid.*, p. (m). According to a MS note in the copy in U.C.N.W. library the author was J. N. Brewer.

92 Hughes, *Cotton*, p. 23. Cf. P. B. Williams, *Tourist's Guide through the County of Caernarvon* (1821), p. 42.

93 Turner's Survey, in Chapter Book.

94 Pring, p. 162.

95 Presumably the congregation at choir services was accommodated in the parochial area. In 1812 it was decided to move the screen to the western crossing arch to make room for more accommodation (C.A., Aug. 4, 1812), but this was not done.

In 1810 the Chapter found itself in a position to finance extensive repairs. The tithes of Llandinam from which the cathedral drew its revenue had been let in 1769 for £230 per annum and in 1790 for £400. The latter lease expired in 1810, and, owing no doubt to the high agricultural prices prevailing during the Napoleonic wars, the property was found to have greatly increased in value. It was now let for £1134, and two-thirds of this sum, £756, fell to the lot of the cathedral.[96] The increase in revenue gave rise to a dispute between the Chapter and the organist which will be recounted later. Here it will suffice to say that as a result of a long drawn out suit in the Chancery Court the Chapter was allowed to spend £2000 of its revenue on repairs to the fabric. The work was put in hand in 1824. John Hall, a Bangor architect, was appointed superintendent surveyor at a salary of two pounds a week, and the contractors were Robert Roberts and Thomas Griffith of Bangor.[97]

Some of the work done in 1824 can still be seen in the tower. The old battlements and pinnacles, built of small stones by then much decayed, were replaced by new work on the old lines, and the tower roof was releaded.[98] It must have been at this time too that the Latin inscription recording the erection of the tower, which according to Browne Willis was "in ancient characters" and when Hyde Hall wrote was "much defaced", was replaced by the present inscription in Roman capitals.[99]

There remained the problem of providing more accommodation. In 1824 the Chapter appointed a committee to consider this question, and in the next year they accepted the plans of John Foster.[100] Foster had recently been appointed architect to the Liverpool Corporation. His Liverpool buildings are "mainly in a cold, correct Grecian style."[101] and he had little

---

96 Pring, p. 154.

97 C.A., Oct. 15, 1823. In 1823 the estimate of Henry Griffith of Liverpool was accepted, but in the accounts payments are recorded as being made to Griffith and Roberts, and in a surviving list of tenders the lowest one is that of Roberts and Griffith of Bangor. (N.L.W., B/DC/114). It appears then that they did the work.

98 In 1951 I observed the date 182- (last figure illegible) scratched on the roof.

99 Browne Willis, p. 21; Hyde Hall, *op. cit.*, p. 156.

100 C.A., Aug. 3, 1824; Jan. 11, 1825.

101 H. M. Colvin, *Biographical Dictionary of English Architects*, p. 212.

sympathy with Gothic;[102] he was therefore not the best choice as architect for the refitting of a medieval cathedral.

The work of altering and refitting the interior followed on that of repair and was the subject of a separate contract, for which tenders were invited in January 1825.[103] Presumably this procedure was dictated by the fact that the Chancery judgment allowed cathedral funds to be used for repairs only, but it must have caused considerable inconvenience, and there seems to have been some lack of co-ordination between the two operations, that of structural repair and that of recasting the interior. Hall took down and rebuilt with new materials the west crossing arch, which had been condemned as dangerous by architects who had previously surveyed the fabric.[104] Foster's plans involved the removal of all four crossing arches, and Hall's new arch was therefore removed immediately after its erection.

The cost of carrying out Foster's plans had to be met by voluntary contributions. By July, 1824, £2147 had been subscribed, a sum which it was stated would be fully adequate.[105] In fact the work was contracted for at the sum of £2500, and the final cost was £3252 19s. 6d.[106] The moving spirit in promoting the work and collecting money was J. H. Cotton, precentor and vicar choral, who, according to his biographer, did the work "almost single handed".[107] The major part of the sum required came from the diocese. The bishop headed the subscription list with £150, to which he later added £50, while his wife and his son each contributed £50. Other large subscriptions were those of Cotton himself (£100), Assheton Smith of Vaynol (£100) and the Marquess of Anglesey (£50).[108] The name of the dean, John Warren, is missing from the subscription list, but it appears that he fully associated himself with the work and made some contribution, as is indicated by the Chapter Minute of August 5, 1828:

---

[102] Quentin Hughes, *Seaport* (1964), pp. 87, 145.
[103] *N.W.G.*, Jan. 13, 1825.
[104] N.L.W., B/DC/115; *N.W.G.*, Dec. 13, 1825. The original specification of February, 1824, included the rebuilding of all four crossing arches. *Arch. Camb.*, 1901, p. 193.
[105] N.W.G., July 22, 1824.
[106] *Ibid.*, Aug. 18, 1825; Oct. 18, 1827.
[107] Hughes, *Cotton*, p. 24.
[108] *N.W.G.*, July 22, 1824.

> The Chapter beg to congratulate the Dean on the Completion of the Church and the reopening the Choir for the celebration of Divine Service. Feeling how greatly the Chapter are indebted to the Dean for the superior style in which the Choir has been completed, they beg leave to offer their best Thanks not only for the Decision which has satisfied the Claims of the Proprietors of Seats, the Suggestions which have increased the Comforts and Convenience of the Public in General, and the Taste which has directed the ornamental Parts of the Choir: But also for the Attention with which he has watched over the last and for the Liberality with which he has met the Expenses attendant upon them.

During the repairs and alterations services took place in the National School in Dean Street, which had been opened in 1822. There was evidently some dissatisfaction on the part of the congregation at their long exile. In June of 1825 the *North Wales Gazette* referred to the tardy progress of the alterations: "Whatever demur there may be relative to the enlarging and beautifying of the Quire portion of the building where the English service is performed, there is just cause of complaint on the part of the parishioners to have their portion of the building fitted up for Welsh services."[109] Later in the year the *Gazette* gave further expression to the public dissatisfaction, remarking that the repairs would not be completed in less than three years.[110] The paper's forecast, though it gave offence to Cotton,[111] was not far from the truth. Though the Welsh church was open by September, 1826,[112] the rest of the work was not completed until two years later. In August, 1828, the choir was at last in use again, and on its re-opening, according to the *North Wales Chronicle* (as the local paper was now called), the cathedral "presented a galaxy of beauty and fashion which we are sure the most splendid congregation that ever assembled in Hanover Square could not eclipse, if even it could slightly shadow it."[113]

[109] *N.W.G.*, June 16, 1825.
[110] *Ibid.*, Dec. 1, 1825.
[111] *Ibid.*, Dec. 13, 1825.
[112] *Ibid.*, Sept. 21, 1826.
[113] *N.W.C.*, Aug. 14, 1828.

All trace of the work done to the interior in 1825-28 has since been obliterated, but with the aid of old prints and descriptions and the plan preserved in the Chapter Book[114] it is not difficult to picture the cathedral as it emerged from the drastic treatment to which it had been subjected. The division between choir and parochial church was preserved, and as more space was needed for the former it was pushed westward into the nave. The organ screen was placed in the fifth bay from the west and the Welsh congregation was accommodated in the four western bays of the nave. This part of the church had its own altar in front of the organ screen; it was covered with a crimson cloth, with a cushion at either end, and by way of reredos there was a gilt star. On the north side of the communion rails was the reading desk, on the south the pulpit; beneath the desk sat the parish clerk, beneath the pulpit the churchwardens. Doors on either side of the altar led to the choir, or English church.[115] Immediately to the east of the organ screen were the stalls, with the bishop's throne and pulpit to the east of them, at the western side of the crossing. The chancel and transepts were filled with high pews; the Consistory Court and vestry were housed in the north aisle behind the stalls. The fittings were of stained deal in the Gothic style; there was a flat plaster ceiling, and the four-centred arches on corbels which replaced the old crossing arches were presumably of the same material.

The cathedral authorities and their architect showed small respect for the past. The removal of the seventeenth-century fittings was perhaps inevitable in view of the decision to alter the seating arrangements and the low opinion then held of woodwork of that period.[116] But there can have been little justification for the complete removal of all the medieval crossing arches. Though the western one was, as we have seen, in a dangerous state and the eastern one was found to be equally dangerous when the organ screen was removed,[117] later restorers would probably have succeeded in preserving these as well as the other two arches. But the aim in the 1820's was not to restore in a conservative sense, but to produce a new and uniform interior

[114] N.L.W., B/DC/V, 2, p. 40.
[115] Hughes, *Recollections*, pp. 15-16.
[116] See the uncomplimentary remarks in Storer, p. (k).
[117] N.L.W., B/DC/115.

arrangement and one which would ensure the maximum seating capacity. Unfortunately there was little merit in the new work to compensate for the loss of the old. Scott—and no doubt he voiced the general opinion of the 1860's—had nothing good to say of the cathedral as he found it. It had, he wrote, "gradually sunk to such low estate as to become almost a byeword—no cathedral in the U.K. being equal to it in meanness"; the stalls were "the most execrable gimcrack that ever disgraced a church."[118] What is condemned by one generation often returns to fashion later, but in this case there need be no regrets that nothing remains of the work of the 1820's.

When Cotton succeeded to the Deanery in 1838, the occasion was marked by a presentation made to him of about £300, which he applied to filling the east window with stained glass. The glass remained in position until Scott's restoration; Scott objected to it as out of keeping with the restored choir, and it was removed. It was however preserved; it was distributed between the west window under the tower and the two westernmost windows in the aisles, where it still remains to remind us what glass painting was like before the revival of the art under the influence of the ecclesiological movement.[119]

In the mid-nineteenth century gas lighting was installed in the parochial part of the building. In the eighteenth century there had been no lighting apart from candles on a few nights at Christmastide.[120] With the establishment of two evening services in 1810, one of which would be after dark in the winter months, it became necessary to supply some illumination, and the *North Wales Gazette* reported in November of that year that the cathedral had for the first time been adorned with lights.[121] In 1849 the latest form of lighting was adopted; the sum of £56 13s. 1d. was paid to the Gas Company for supplying

---

118 Scott, *Letter to the Dean and Chapter*, 1866.

119 Hughes, *Cotton*, pp. 84-5, 155-6. I believe the glass to be the work of David Evans of Shrewsbury, but cannot now trace my authority for this ascription. The figures in the main lights were Moses, Aaron, David and Solomon, the four evangelists, St. Peter and St. Paul. As there are two tiers of five lights in the east window and three lights in each of the windows at the west end, one of the figures had to be jettisoned. The choice fell on Solomon.

120 Browne Willis, p.31.

121 *N.W.G.* Nov. 15, 1810.

fittings and gas to the "Welsh Church."[122] A few years later a restoration of limited scope was undertaken. In 1857 the interior was cleaned and renovated and the choir given a new roof of oak, from the designs of Henry Kennedy of Bangor, the work being financed from the income of the Precentorship which was kept vacant when Cotton succeeded to the Deanery; at the same time, at the expense of the bishop (Bethell) a new altar, pulpit, reading desk and throne were installed.[123]

Even with these improvements however the cathedral did not satisfy the liturgical and aesthetic standards of the period, and when James Vincent succeeded to the Deanery in 1862 it was decided to subject the building to a new and radical restoration. Sir Gilbert Scott was called in to advise; as the leading architect of the day and one who had already been entrusted with the restoration of a number of cathedrals he was the obvious choice. He reported to the Dean and Chapter in March, 1866, suggesting two alternative courses.[124] The first was to limit the work to a thorough repair of the fabric and "the worthy fitting up and seemly decoration of the interior." The second was to restore or partially reconstruct the choir, transepts and chapter house "in such a style as is indicated by their few remaining fragments." By this he meant the buttresses on the south transept which had survived the reconstruction of *c.* 1500 and which he particularly admired—"I used to say," he wrote elsewhere, "that Bangor cathedral contained nothing worth seeing but three buttresses."[125] His second scheme, he went on to say, was a departure from the conservative treatment which he usually advocated, but might be justified in the circumstances. He did not positively recommend either course. There was room, he said, for differences of opinion; "it is a question between redeeming the church of its mean character and infringing in some degree on its authentic architectural history." He raised the question of a central tower; if his second scheme, which involved some historical loss, were adopted, he thought they should compensate

[122] C.A., Aug. 7, 1849.

[123] *Ibid.*, Aug. 7, 1855; Dec. 3, 1855; Aug. 5, 1857; *N.W.C.* July 25, 1857. The financing of the work from funds subject to the judgment of the Chancery Court involved a long correspondence. C.A. Nov. 18, 1840; Dec. 4, 1847; Feb. 15, 1848; March 19, 1849; Aug. 5, 1851; Aug. 3, 1852; Aug. 2, 1853.

[124] *Letter to the Dean and Chapter*, 1866.

[125] Scott, *Personal and Professional Recollections*, 1879, p. 316.

for the loss by making the work a really noble one and completing it with a tower.

In April, 1866, a public meeting was held, a subscription list opened and a restoration committee formed.[126] The committee decided on Scott's second scheme, and by 1868 enough money had been subscribed to justify a beginning. Tenders were invited for the first stage of the work, the restoration and partial rebuilding of transepts and crossing and the construction of the central tower to the ridge of the roof. The contractors were Messrs. Beauland of Bradford, who tendered at the sum of £10,477. This was followed by the restoration of the choir and the building of the organ chamber. The structural work on the choir was executed by Beauland for £3,075 12s. 0d.; the decoration, including the stained glass in the east window, was the work of Clayton and Bell and was paid for by Lord Penrhyn.[127] The cost of the organ chamber, for which the contractor was Richard Parry of Menai Bridge, was £1,245, and a new organ, by Messrs. Hill, cost £880.[128] The total sum expended by 1873 was £19,430 2s. 0d.[129] In that year the cathedral was reopened. The old organ screen was removed from the nave and some temporary repairs made, but otherwise nothing was done to this part of the building until 1879, when the subscription list was reopened and work on the nave begun; at the same time the rebuilding of the block to the north of the choir was completed by the addition of the vestry and chapter house. The contractor for this final stage of the work was Thompson of Peterborough and the cost was £9,184.[130] It was completed in 1880. By then Gilbert Scott was dead, and his son, J. Oldrid Scott, who had been in his father's office and had doubtless helped with the earlier stages, was in charge; it is convenient however to refer to the restoration as a whole as the work of the elder Scott.

Scott's plans involved a virtually complete rebuilding of the transepts, and in the course of the work discoveries were made

---

[126] For details of the Scott restoration see the Restoration Minute Book, N.L.W., B/DC/V.6.
[127] The glass in the south choir window is probably also by Clayton and Bell.
[128] The organ was repaired and enlarged in 1897.
[129] N.L.W., B/DC/9.
[130] P.P. 1884-5 XXI, Cathedral Commission, Final Report, 1885, p. 35.

which must have seemed to justify the policy adopted. Considerable fragments were found in the walls which enabled him to reconstruct the original windows to his own satisfaction and that of subsequent antiquaries. He was also able to restore the original east and west arches of the transepts from remains that he found, partly *in situ*, though in the north transept he did not perpetuate the old level of the bases, which owing to the slope of the ground had been lower than that of the crossing. He found the bases of the responds of the crossing arches and fragments of the arches themselves, and followed them "in the main, subject to some additions necessary for their stability." He also found part of their capitals, but they were so thin that he did not venture to use them in the piers of the crossing but found a place for them in the smaller arches, for which he found no caps.[131] He intended to rebuild the chapel on the south side of the choir,[132] but funds did not extend to this, and the reopened arch in the east wall of the transept had to be blocked and has remained so since.

In dealing with the choir Scott was more conservative. It showed, as he put it, "evidences of the threefold history of the church" which he did not wish to remove,[133] and as the remains of thirteenth-century work which came to light here were, in his words, "too plain to form part of the beautiful work of the time of Edward I,"[134] there was no historical justification for bringing the choir into line with the transepts. This did not however prevent him from adding buttresses and a corbel table like those of the south transept, the buttresses being based on fragments found in the wall of the transept, which must originally have come not from the choir but from the south chapel.[135]

The buildings on the north of the choir cannot pretend to be, except as regards style, a restoration of the original structure. As we have seen, the work was done in two stages. The area immediately to the east of the transept was made into an organ chamber, opening into the transept by the restored medieval arch and into the choir by a new arch on the site of the old

---

131 Scott, *Second Report*, p. 18.
132 *Ibid.*, p. 31. After the First World War there was a proposal to rebuild this chapel as a war memorial, but it came to nothing. C.A., May 5, 1919.
133 Scott, *Second Report*, p. 30.
134 *Ibid.*, p. 18.
135 Scott was himself doubtful about this procedure. *Ibid.*, p. 31.

arched tomb; to this was added the two-storey building to the east, comprising vestry with chapter house and library above. The nave was receiled and refloored. The tracery of some of the aisle windows, the heads of which had been filled with what Scott called "debased" tracery, probably dating from Bishop Skevington's rebuilding, was restored, and battlements were added over the clerestorey.[136]

The lofty central tower and spire which Scott designed never rose above the ridge of the roofs. After a few years it was observed that the joints at the apices of the tower arches had opened by half an inch. Oldrid Scott attributed this to contraction of the Portland cement, and considered that it would be safe to complete the tower.[137] The Chapter however decided to get an independent opinion from Francis Stevenson, chief engineer of the London and North Western Railway, who thought the cracks might be due to subsidence of the foundations and advised that borings be taken.[138] This was carried out in 1892, and the engineer's report was evidently thought sufficiently discouraging to preclude the completion of the tower, for which in any case no funds were available.[139] This is not entirely to be regretted, for whatever the merits of Scott's design the tower would have been grossly out of proportion with the nave and west tower. Even apart from the central tower the choir and transepts as reconstructed by Scott do not fit happily to the nave, and the building as it left his hands is less homogeneous than it previously was. Nonetheless he certainly gave new dignity to the interior, and it might well be maintained that this was the first occasion since the early fourteenth century when work was done on the cathedral which was by contemporary standards of the best quality.

Scott's plans involved the abandonment of the old division into cathedral and parish church. He placed the stalls in the choir, leaving the transepts free for congregational use in addition to the nave. The stalls were not completed until 1879, when a bishop's throne, the gift of the freemasons, was also

---

136 There may have been battlements originally, but old engravings show that there had been none since the eighteenth century.
137 C.A. June 24, 1889.
138 *Ibid.*, Aug. 6, 1891.
139 Report on loose sheet at C.A. Aug. 6, 1891.

erected. But it was evidently found that the placing of the stalls was unsatisfactory, and in 1908 they were moved to their present position under the tower. At the same time additional stalls, a close copy of the existing ones, were erected in the choir, and a screen was placed under the western crossing arch ; this was in accordance with the intentions of Gilbert Scott, who had proposed to erect a "noble open screen"[140], though under the eastern rather than the western arch. All this work was a memorial to Lord Penrhyn; it was carried out by Thompson of Peterborough to the designs of Oldrid Scott.[141]

It remains to record the further embellishments which accompanied or followed Scott's restoration. The pulpit, designed by Gilbert Scott, is a memorial to Morris Williams (died 1874). The reredos, presented in 1881 by Mrs. Elizabeth Atcherley Symes of Gorphwysfa in memory of her brother, was designed by Oldrid Scott.[142] The lectern dates from 1905 and was presented by the family of Dean Lewis in his memory.[143] In 1885 Mrs. Symes presented the stained glass window in the south transept, the work of the Munich firm of Mayer, in memory of Dean Edwards.[144] The stained glass in the south aisle window immediately to the east of the door dates from 1905 and the third window from the door from the following year; the former is a memorial to Dean Pryce, the latter to Bishop Campbell. Between them is one later in date (1929) in memory of Canon E. T. Davies.[145] The series of five windows in the north aisle, the work of Powell and Grant, dates from 1911 and was installed as a result of a legacy from Miss H. S. Hughes of Brynymenai.[146]

Little was done to the cathedral in the period between the wars, the most important work being connected with heating and lighting. In 1934 the gas coronae, dating from the Scott restoration, which are a conspicuous feature of the interior as

[140] Scott, Second Report, p. 31.
[141] C.A., April 3, 1907; Feb. 11, 1908. Bangor Diocesan Calendar 1909, p. 305.
[142] C.A., Aug. 24, 1881; Nov. 28, 1881.
[143] *Ibid.*, Feb. 14, 1905.
[144] *Ibid.*, Aug. 4 and 5, 1885; *Byegones relating to Wales* 1886-7, p. 61.
[145] C.A., March 20, 1905; Feb. 1, July 31, 1906; Feb. 16, 1928; July 31, 1929. The Campbell window is by Burlison and Grylls, and the Pryce window may be assumed to be by the same artists. The Davies window is by the same firm (Grylls and Co.).
[146] *Ibid.*, Aug. 9, 1910; Jan. 13, July 31, 1911.

shown in old photographs, gave place to electric light fittings, and in 1939 a new heating system was installed.

The question of the completion of the central tower which had lain dormant since the 1890's was reopened by the bequest in 1945 by Mr. A. T. King, of Caernarvon, of £30,000 for the erection of a tower. His wish was that this should be on the lines of that of Selby Abbey; if the completion of the tower should prove impracticable, the bequest was to be transferred to to the Representative Body for the benefit of the Church in Wales. Once more consulting engineers were called in to advise, and once more their reports were discouraging. An alternative scheme was produced by the cathedral architect, Mr. A. D. R. Caroe, for finishing off the existing stump with a spire much lighter than a tower of the type envisaged by Mr. King, but this ran into difficulties. There were doubts whether the foundations would bear even this, and the scheme was contested as not in accordance with the terms of the bequest. Though the decision of the Chancery Court confirmed that the testator's wish would be fulfilled under the alternative scheme, the Chapter decided in February, 1950, not to proceed with it. The bequest therefore reverted to the Representative Body, which however allowed it to be used for the benefit of the cathedral. It was thus possible to put in hand some much needed repairs. In 1951-3 the nave and aisles were reroofed with copper[147] and this was followed by the releading of the south transept (1958-9) and the choir (1963-4) and the reroofing in copper of the tower (1966). The interior of nave and aisles was replastered in 1953-4.

A grant from the King bequest, with an anonymous gift of £6,000, made it possible to carry out a complete reconstruction of the organ. The work was done by the John Compton Organ Company and completed in 1954. The old organ chamber was considered to be far too cramped to hold the reconstructed organ, and while the Solo and Choir organs remained in the chamber, the Great, Swell and Pedal organs were moved to the north transept. At the same time the console was transferred to the south transept.

In 1942 a legacy was received from Miss M. L. D. Williams for the purpose of erecting a hanging rood over the choir screen.

---

[147] At the same time the parapet of the south aisle was raised.

Owing to war conditions it was impossible to implement the bequest until 1950, when the rood, designed by Mr. Caroe, was installed; the figures were carved by Harold Youngman, and the rest of the work executed by A. Robinson. In 1944 a gift was received from Miss Watts for the erection of a reredos in the Lady Chapel in the south transept; the work, designed by Mr. Caroe, was carried out in 1950. The mural painting in the arch above the reredos, the work of Brian Thomas, was dedicated in 1955 and is a memorial to Dean Griffith Roberts. The screen at the east end of the north aisle, a memorial to Dean James, dates from 1954 and the corresponding one on the south side, a memorial to Sir Hugh Corbet Vincent, from 1960 Both are from the designs of Mr. Caroe. In 1960 certain re-arrangements were made in the nave, including the erection of a nave altar.

The most interesting recent acquisition is the "Mostyn Christ", a figure of Christ carved in oak, of late fifteenth or early sixteenth century date, which was deposited on permanent loan in the cathedral by Lord Mostyn in 1953. It is of a type rarely found; Christ is represented before the crucifixion, seated on a rock, bound and wearing a crown of thorns. There is no record of how it came into the possession of the Mostyn family; the tradition is that it was originally in Llanrwst church or Maenan abbey, and it has been identified with what was described in 1684 as a figure of the crucifixion "over the timber arch near the rood loft" at Llanrwst and in 1735, if the reference is to the same figure, as an image of St. Grwst kept in the rood loft. It does not however represent the crucifixion, and its original position was evidently not in a rood loft. There is therefore much to be said for the theory recently advanced that it should rather be identified with the figure of Christ which was set up in the garden of Rhuddlan priory in 1518 and is described in a Welsh poem in terms which agree well with the character of the figure now in the Cathedral.[148]

In 1965 an appeal was launched for a sum of £125,000 in order to carry out repairs and improvements, to provide additional income and to meet other needs of the cathedral. In the next

---

[148] See *Bulletin of the Board of Celtic Studies* 21 (1965), pp. 236-42, and, for earlier discussions, *Arch. Camb.* 1943, p. 231; 1944, p. 139.

year a start was made on the exterior. The stump of Scott's central tower was finished off with battlements and a pyramidal cap, from the designs of Mr. Caroe, and this work, completed in 1967, was followed by the reroofing of the north transept. Thus at the time of writing the reroofing which was begun in 1951 has been completed and the problem of the central tower, which had been with the cathedral for nearly a century, has found a satisfactory solution.

CHAPTER 2

THE CHAPTER

Bangor is a cathedral "of the old foundation", that is a secular cathedral whose constitution was unaffected by the dissolution of the monasteries. The old *clas* developed under Norman influence into a Chapter of canons headed by a dean. There is no record of how and when this development took place; all we can say is that a dean is first mentioned in 1162,[1] a dean and chapter in 1236.[2] The earliest list of the chapter is that given in the *Taxatio* of Pope Nicholas of 1291.[3] It shows a dean, three archdeacons (of Bangor, Anglesey and Merioneth) and seven canons. The three dignitaries, Precentor, Chancellor and Treasurer, are not found earlier than 1504, when they appear in the return made to Archbishop Warham.[4] In the sixteenth-century lists of the chapter we find five canons in addition to the three archdeacons and the three dignitaries, making with the dean a total of twelve;[5] by the latter part of the century the two canons with separate endowments were distinguished by the titles of Prebendary of Llanfair and Prebendary of Penmynydd.

There were no cathedral statutes, and precedence was therefore a matter of custom rather than ordinance.[6] All lists place the Archdeacons, in the order Bangor, Anglesey, Merioneth, immediately after the dean. In 1504 the dignitaries appear in the order Chancellor, Treasurer, Precentor, and in 1561 in what was the usual order in English cathedrals, Precentor, Chancellor, Treasurer. In the latter year the two prebendaries are placed before the dignitaries. In the post-Restoration period this was the accepted order, and among the dignitaries

---

1 According to a document of unknown origin, quoted in Browne Willis, p. 184, "Iago ap Beli rex decanatu ecclesiam dotavit". But a dean at so early a date (early seventh century) seems hardly credible.

2 *C.P.R.*, 1232-1247, p. 149.

3 *Taxatio P. Nicholai* (1802), p. 290; Browne Willis, p. 200.

4 A. I. Pryce, *Diocese of Bangor in the Sixteenth Century*, App. A. In 1450 John Graystock held the prebend of Llanfihangel y Traethau (*C.P.L.*, X, p. 74), but whether this was then, as it later was, attached to the Treasurership is not clear.

5 In the list of 1561 there are thirteen in all, perhaps because the prebend of Llanfair was then held by a layman.

6 I am indebted to Dr. J. W. James for a memorandum on this point.

the Treasurer came first. This order appears to have been based on financial considerations, the two endowed prebends ranking above the dignities, while among the dignities the only endowed one, the Treasurership, had precedence. The same ranking is reflected in the placing of the stalls as fixed at the Restoration. Whereas the normal arrangement in secular cathedrals is for the Dean and the three other dignitaries to sit at the four corners of the choir, with the precentor at the west end of the north side, opposite to the Dean, at Bangor the order from west to east was on the south side Dean, Archdeacon of Merioneth, Prebendary of Llanfair, Treasurer, Chancellor, Precentor, and on the north Archdeacon of Bangor, Archdeacon of Anglesey, Prebendary of Penmynydd, Canonicus Primus, Secundus, Tertius.[7] The present arrangement is the same except that on the north the canon in residence sits in the westernmost stall, with the Archdeacon of Bangor next to him, and two additional canons, Quartus and Quintus, have been added at the east, on the north and south sides respectively. Thus the side which every chorister knows as Cantoris is not at Bangor that of the cantor, or precentor.

According to the Taxatio of Pope Nicholas the total revenue of the cathedral clergy was then £133,[8] the income of individuals ranging from £20 (Dean and Archdeacon of Anglesey) to £3, but no information is given about the sources of the revenue. The Chapter also had £21 as their half share of certain temporalities then held by them in common with the bishop.[9] In the fourteenth century we hear of a prebend worth £15 and another worth £10, and in 1446 the Archdeaconry of Anglesey was worth £40.[10] In the *Valor Ecclesiasticus* of 1535 we find the dean possessed of a net income of £22 17s. 2d. derived from the rectories of Gyffin and Llanfihangel Esceifiog with Llanffinan, with a small additional sum from glebe in Bangor and a share of

7 According to John Ellis in a letter to Browne Willis of 1719, "Precedency is not much regarded, but we reckon it according to everyone's stall beginning with the Dean and so on by sides." That is, the holder of each stall on the south was followed by the holder of the corresponding stall on the north. Bodleian MS Jesus College 115, p. 40.

8 *Taxatio P. Nicholai*, p. 290. The total is given as £233, but the individual sums add up to £133.

9 *Ibid.*, p. 292; *Record of Caernarvon*, p. 229.

10 *C.P.L.*, III., p. 182; *Reg. Simon Langham* (Canterbury and York Society, 1956), p. 49; *C.P.L.* IX, p. 576.

cathedral oblations. The Archdeacon of Bangor had the rectories of Llannor with Denio, Llandegai and Caerhun which, with fees, glebe and oblations, gave him £48 6s. 1d.; the Archdeacon of Anglesey, most of whose income came from the rectories of Amlwch with Llanwenllwyfo and Llangristiolus with Cerrigceinwen, had £58 10s. 6d., and the Archdeacon of Merioneth, who held the rectory of Llandudno, £13 3s. 3d. The Treasurer held a portion of the rectory of Llanfihangel y Traethau, which with glebe and oblations brought him no more than 18s. 8d. (The ownership of this benefice was then in dispute; before and after this date the whole of it belonged to the Treasurer.[11]) Two of the canons, though not given distinguishing titles, held the prebends of Llanfair and Penmynydd respectively; the former (the rectory of Llanfair Dyffryn Clwyd)[12] was worth £39, the latter £8 5s. 6d. The others, apart from two who were non-resident, shared in the common fund derived from glebe and oblations, which brought them in no more than from 3s. 4d. to 4s. each. What happened to the glebe is not clear; in 1561 the income of the common fund was said to be derived solely from oblations and to amount at the most to 40s. a year in all.[13] By the eighteenth century oblations were a thing of the past, and the unendowed stalls were paradoxically known as "nihil prebends".[14]

In the absence of statutes or other evidence it is impossible to say what were the rules about residence in the Middle Ages or what efforts were made to enforce it; but it is clear that at Bangor as elsewhere in the later Middle Ages many members of the Chapter were non-resident. Cathedral prebends were commonly bestowed on those engaged in royal or ecclesiastical administration or on well placed and influential clergy. Bangor was no exception; prebends in Wales were not reserved for the Welsh clergy. In 1309 Ralph de Melton was granted a prebend at Bangor on the resignation of William de Melton, and in 1352 Peter de Gildesburgh exchanged his Bangor prebend with

[11] *Valor Ecclesiasticus* IV, p. 417. In 1431 we hear of the "canonry of Lanbyhatigellytrach" (*sic*) worth £20 (*C.P.L.* VIII p. 334); in 1648 the rectory of Llanfihangel y Traethau with the chapel of Llandecwyn, value £42 3s. 0d., belonged to the Treasurer. Browne Willis, p. 287.

[12] This endowment was originally secured in 1386. See p. 13, n. 19.

[13] Browne Willis, p. 263.

[14] *Ibid.*, p. 42.

Peter de Wotton, prebendary of the collegiate church of Tamworth; all four are described as king's clerks.[15] Robert de Tresk, who obtained a prebend at Bangor in 1344, was described in the following year as having laboured in the Roman court for twelve years.[16] Such men often collected a large number of benefices. William de Melton was rector of Hornsea in the diocese of York, and held two other benefices as well as prebends at Dublin and Westbury (diocese of Worcester).[17] Peter de Gildesburgh was archdeacon of Totnes, canon and prebendary of Exeter, Lincoln and Llandaff, and in addition to these and other benefices received a papal provision to a prebend at Hereford in 1349.[18] Robert de Tresk in 1345 petitioned for an additional prebend when he already held prebends at Bangor and Heytesbury (Salisbury diocese) and had received a papal provision to one at Salisbury.[19] In the returns of pluralists made in 1366 in response to a decree of Pope Urban V we find the names of William Loring, beneficed in the diocese of Lincoln and holding a prebend at Bangor, half the rectory of Llandinam and a canonry with expectation of a prebend at Salisbury,[20] and of Ralph Ringstede, who in addition to his Bangor prebend held a vicarage in Exeter diocese and prebends in Exeter cathedral and at Heytesbury.[21] It can hardly be an accident that he bears the same name as Thomas Ringstede, bishop of Bangor.

It is not until Tudor times that we have clear evidence as to the extent of non-residence. In the *Valor Ecclesiasticus* two of the canons are said to be non-resident and therefore in receipt of no income from the common fund. As this was so small there was little incentive to reside, and it is perhaps surprising that the others canons not otherwise endowed qualified to receive their share. The Dean, the Archdeacons and the Treasurer may be

---

15 *C.P.R.* 1307-13, p. 176; *ibid.*, 1350-54, p. 212. Cf. *ibid.* 1388-92, p. 156.
16 *C.P.P.*, I, p. 105.
17 *C.P.L.*, II, p. 42 (1308).
18 *C.P.L.* III, p. 314.
19 *C.P.P.* I, p. 105.
20 *Reg. Simon Langham* (Canterbury and York Society, 1956), p. 49; *C.P.R.* 1385-89, p. 221; *Arch. Camb.* 1922, p. 102. On his death Loring bequeathed a chalice and some books to Bangor. (*Reg. Henry Chichele* (Canterbury and York Society, 1937), II, p. 80). He was a brother of Sir Nigel Loring, steward of the Black Prince's household. *Ibid.*, p. 662.
21 *Reg. Simon Langham*, pp. 75-6.

assumed to have been resident since they received their share of oblations; the holders of the benefices of Llanfair and Penmynydd, who did not receive a share, may be assumed to have been non-resident. In 1561, when the Chapter appears to have been largely, if not wholly, Welsh in composition, the Dean resided in Bangor; of the Archdeacons one, Edmund Meyrick, was described as a student at Oxford, another (John Salisbury, suffragan bishop of Thetford and Chancellor of Lincoln) divided his time between Norwich and Lincoln, and the third was resident either in Bangor or in the diocese. The Prebendary of Llanfair, John Gwyn was described as "remaining at churches in London", which appears to be a euphemism for practising as a lawyer;[22] the Prebendary of Penmynydd divided his time between Penmynydd and a benefice in Oxford diocese. The Precentor lived in Anglesey, the Chancellor in London and the Treasurer in Bangor. Of the other canons two resided in Bangor and two in the diocese.[23] This is the information given in a return made to the Archbishop of Canterbury. It needs to be read along with the contemporary returns to visitations by the diocesan, which show that only one member of the Chapter besides the Dean was permanently resident.[24] In 1587 the Dean and two prebendaries were resident and "all the rest be abroad", and in 1617, in addition to the Dean, the Archdeacon of Bangor, the Chancellor and the Precentor resided "all or most of the year".[25]

The Reformation brought no change to the cathedral constitution or to the endowments of the Chapter. Since five of the Chapter including the Dean are believed to have been ejected under Mary on account of their being married, it may be assumed that in this respect at any rate the Reformation was welcomed at the cathedral.[26] Under Elizabeth I we find a new

---

[22] See *Dictionary of Welsh Biography*. John Gwyn was a layman.

[23] Browne Willis, pp. 262-3.

[24] Visitations. William Powell, Maurice Powell, Moythe (1560) and Evans (1567) state that only the Dean and Moythe are resident. Myrian (1560) and Bulkeley (1567) state that only the Dean is.

[25] Visitations. Burches and Mason 1587. Mason, 1617.

[26] Those deprived were Robert Evans, Dean, reinstated 1557; John Salisbury, Archdeacon of Merioneth, reinstated 1559; Lewis Newburgh, Treasurer; David Lloyd, Prebendary of Penmynydd; Hugh ap Robert, canon. Browne Willis, pp. 126, 151, 155, 176; Pryce, *Diocese of Bangor in the* 16*th Century*, p. 13.

emphasis on preaching. In the 1560's only the Dean, and occasionally the Archdeacon of Bangor, preached.[27] In 1576 Archbishop Grindal made a visitation and drew up a scheme under which the Dean was to preach on Christmas and Easter days, and there was to be a sermon on the first Sunday of each month, the Archdeacons of Bangor and Anglesey and the Prebendary of Llanfair each preaching once a quarter. In addition to this the other prebendaries having a church or churches annexed to their prebend were to preach once a year;[28] in this category would come the Archdeacon of Merioneth, the Prebendary of Penmynydd and the Treasurer, who were presumably allotted lighter duty in view of their smaller incomes. This scheme if it was ever put into operation appears to have lapsed by 1632 when Prebendary J. Griffith stated "I never knew any sett method for preaching in the said cathedrall."[29]

Cathedral Chapters, which had escaped the rapacity of Henry VIII, did not escape the far more radical reformation which was attempted a century or so later. In 1648 Parliament abolished Deans and Chapters, and in the next year sequestrated their property in order to pay for preaching ministers and schoolmasters. A survey of Bangor property made in this connection gave the Chapter incomes as follows: Dean £107 10s. 6d.; Archdeacon of Bangor £190 2s. 6d.; Archdeacon of Anglesey £212 4s. 0d.; Archdeacon of Merioneth £61 13s. 4d.; Prebendary of Llanfair £151; Prebendary of Penmynydd £39; Treasurer £43 3s. 0d.[30] These endowments were recovered at the Restoration; the Chapter was reconstituted and a new order of preaching drawn up, which gave the cathedral one sermon every Sunday, a fine of 6s. 8d. being imposed for failure to perform the duty.[31] The bishop was now a member of the Chapter. In 1592 he had assumed *in commendam* the valuable archdeaconry of Anglesey. In 1669 he added that of Bangor, and both were permanently annexed to the bishopric by the Act of 1685. With two votes in Chapter the Bishop was therefore an influential figure in the affairs of the cathedral.

27 Visitations. William Powell, Moythe, Myrian, Maurice Powell (1560), Evans, Bulkeley (1567).
28 Strype, *Edmund Grindal* (1821), pp. 316-8.
29 Visitations. Griffiths, 1632.
30 Browne Willis, pp. 283-7.
31 Browne Willis, p. 289.

The earliest extant Chapter Book opens in 1680, and from that date onwards it is possible to follow the details of capitular business. Chapter meetings, which all members were supposed to attend, though they seldom did, were held at no fixed date until 1769, when it was decided to hold an annual chapter on the first Tuesday in August, a date which was altered in 1802 to the first Thursday after the second day in August;[32] other meetings were held as required. In the later seventeenth century one meeting a year was generally found sufficient; as the eighteenth century progressed, meetings became rather more frequent and in the last two decades of the century the average was about three a year.

Griffith Williams, who resumed possession of the deanery at the Restoration, combined the post with the Irish bishopric of Ossory, and was presumably seldom seen in Bangor; and the same may be said of his successor William Lloyd (later to become famous as one of the seven bishops tried in 1688), who from 1676 was vicar of St. Martin-in-the-Fields in London as well as Dean of Bangor. Humphrey Humphreys, appointed Dean in 1680 rebuilt the deanery,[33] and from his time on the deans resided there. There were no other capitular residences, and if, as was sometimes the case, members of the Chapter lived in Bangor they occupied private houses. The majority of the Chapter in the post-Restoration period were beneficed in the diocese, but it was not uncommon for the bishop to present his relatives to the prebends and the endowed Treasurership, and as the bishops from 1715 onwards were all Englishmen the presentees would be beneficed outside Wales. Bishop Zachary Pearce was an exception to the general rule. "He established in himself," we read, "a resolution of conferring Welch preferment or benefices only on Welchmen; to this resolution he adhered in defiance of influence or importunity. He twice gave away the Deanery and bestowed many benefices; but always chose for his patronage the natives of the country, whatever might be the murmurs of his relations or the disappointment of his chaplains.[34] Others were not so scrupulous. Bishop Baker made his brother Nicholas

[32] C.A., Aug. 8, 1769; Aug. 5, 1802. These regulations were changed more than once later in the nineteenth century.

[33] Browne Willis, p. 42. William Lloyd contributed to the cost.

[34] *Lives of Pocock, Pearce, Norton and Skelton*, 1816, I, p. 420.

Treasurer;[35] Bishop Egerton gave the Treasurership to his son and the prebend of Penmynydd to his kinsman Egerton Leigh.[36] Bishop Warren made one nephew dean and another prebendary of Llanfair. The appointment of Robert Foote as Treasurer was also due to Warren; he wanted to do something more for his nephew the dean, so he made a bargain with Foote by which the latter vacated his prebend at Lichfield in favour of Dean Warren, taking in exchange the Treasurership at Bangor.[37] C. P. Layard, prebendary of Penmynydd from 1799 to 1803, does not seem to have had any family connection with Warren; perhaps it was enough that his brother-in-law was a duke.[38] Warren's nepotism went still further. He presented another nephew, Charles Warren, to the chancellorship of the diocese, and yet another, a youth called Gunning, at the time of his appointment both a minor and insane, as Registrar of the Consistory Court.[39] The practice of providing for the bishop's relatives was not extinct in the nineteenth century, and the worthy Bishop Majendie saw no objection to presenting his young son to the prebend of Penmynydd. There was nothing new and nothing unusual about such nepotism; but it bore hardly on the Welsh clergy at a time when the absence of Welshmen on the episcopal bench reduced the prospects of preferment elsewhere.[40]

Nepotistic appointments could turn out better than might have been expected. The appointment of Bishop Warren's nephew and namesake as dean at the age of twenty-seven was on the face of it scandalous. As an undergraduate at Cambridge he had been idle and dissipated.[41] One of his escapades resulted in his being wounded with a sword on the forehead by a man who was trying to blackmail him, and he used to wear his hair over his

[35] *D.N.B.*, *s.v.* William Baker.

[36] For the Egerton and Leigh families see *The Complete Peerage* under Bridgwater and Burke's *Landed Gentry* under Leigh formerly of West Hall, High Leigh.

[37] Shôn Gwialan. *Letter to the Right Reverend Dr. Warren*, 1796, p. 21 n.

[38] A. J. C. Hare, *Life and Letters of Frances Baroness Bunsen*, 1894, I, p. 45. It may be relevant that the duke (of Ancaster) owned land in Caernarvonshire (the former Wynn estate of Gwydir).

[39] Shôn Gwialan, *op. cit.*, p. 20; *The Trial of the Cause of the King versus the Bishop of Bangor*, 1796, p. 93.

[40] Even in the eighteenth century however Bangor clergy sometimes did well for themselves. Hugh Wynne when he died in 1754 was prebendary of Salisbury and of St. Paul's as well as Archdeacon of Merioneth, and Peter Maurice, Dean from 1727 to 1750, was also a canon of Winchester.

[41] Gunning, *Reminiscences of Cambridge*, 1855, II, pp. 51-3.

forehead to conceal the scar. His moral failings were well known in Bangor, and "Shôn Gwialan", the pseudonymous author of a pamphlet against Bishop Warren, describes him as one "whose sensual frailties would have disqualified him for a curacy in any diocese in the Principality".[42] Nonetheless he proved a reasonably good dean. Henry Gunning, to whom we owe our knowledge of his Cambridge career, after losing sight of him for some years met him again when on a holiday in North Wales. He was invited to meet the Dean of Bangor and found that he was none other than the Jack Warren he had known at Cambridge, now settled down to clerical respectability. "He performed," says Gunning, "all his clerical duties with great correctness and propriety and was respected by all around him".

It was Warren who guided the Chapter in the dispute with Dr. Pring which will be recounted later. But the leading figure in the life of the cathedral from 1810 to his death in 1862 was J. H. Cotton, who served for twenty-eight years as Vicar and Precentor and twenty-four as Dean. He was a son of the Dean of Chester and so would have been well known to Bishop Majendie when the latter was Bishop of Chester. In 1809 Majendie appointed him to the vicarage of Derwen in Denbighshire, then in his gift, which he exchanged in the next year for the vicarage of Bangor. In the same year he married one of the bishop's daughters. The appointment of an Englishman closely connected with the bishop might well have seemed another example of the familiar nepotism. But Cotton proved himself an exemplary clergyman. He identified himself with his adopted country, taught himself Welsh and took a leading part in all diocesan and parochial activities, particularly in the promotion of education. Genial, generous and devoted to his calling, he was much loved for his goodness of heart. So far as the church in Bangor adapted itself to the rapid change and expansion that took place in the nineteenth century it was largely due to his efforts.

Cathedral establishments, which had survived intact from the Middle Ages and which supported so many clerics who apparently did nothing to earn the money they received, came under strong criticism in the early nineteenth century. It was

---

[42] Shôn Gwialan, *op. cit.*, p. 14; cf. p. 36.

generally recognised that the time had come for a more equitable and rational distribution of the church's resources, and a new reformation, one of organisation rather than doctrine, began with Peel's appointment of the Ecclesiastical Commission in 1835. This had been preceded by a commission of enquiry into ecclesiastical revenues, whose report issued in 1835 revealed a pattern of incomes which it would have been hard to justify. At Bangor the bishop was decidedly well off with a net income of £4,464,[43] contrasting with Llandaff's £924 and, to mention only two not unimportant English dioceses, Exeter's £2,713 and Gloucester's £2,282. The Dean's income of £858 was a good one in a diocese where the average income of incumbents was £252,[44] and the two prebendaries, Warren's nephew and Majendie's son, whose sinecure posts brought them £459 and £386 respectively, were obvious targets for reform. The Treasurership was now worth £91, and the Precentor received £73 from Llandinam in addition to the £419 from the Bangor tithes and the £46 from Llandinam which he received as Vicar Choral.

The general plan of the Ecclesiastical Commissioners was to reduce cathedral establishments by restricting residentiary canonries to four and abolishing endowed non-residentiary prebends, the incomes of which, on the death of the existing holders, were to be vested in the Commissioners. The scheme however was based on the English cathedrals with their often large and wealthy establishments; it was recognised that Wales, where the capitular revenues were small and there were no residentiaries and no daily choral services, presented peculiar problems and would have to be treated separately from England. The English cathedrals were dealt with in an Act of 1840, those of Wales in one of 1843.[45] The Commissioners' first plan for Bangor was a drastic one. They proposed to unite the two archdeaconries held by the bishop into one, detach it from the bishopric and join it with the deanery, to give the Archdeacon of Merioneth an additional endowment from a suppressed prebend and to confine the Chapter to two canons who would perform

[43] See Clerical Guide, 1836, tables I and II. All figures given here are net. The gross income was in many cases considerably higher.
[44] The Ecclesiastical Commissioners reduced the Dean's income to £700.
[45] Vict. 3 and 4, Cap. CXIII (1840); Vict. 6 and 7, Cap. LXXVII (1843).

the same functions as the existing vicars.[46] This scheme was modified in the Act of 1843. The cathedral was allowed to retain its full-time dean, and the two archdeaconries, that of Merioneth and that formed from the two previously held by the bishop, were to be annexed to residentiary canonries. Of these there were to be four in all; their holders, who were allotted a salary of £350, were each to reside for three months in the year, and the cathedral was permitted to apply its funds to building a house for them.

The new constitution took some time to come into operation and did not do so without difficulties The Law Officers of the Crown ruled that the Act of 1843 could not be carried into effect until the Chapter had been reduced to four. By 1853 this had come about.[47] The bishop duly surrendered his archdeaconries in 1844, the precentorship had been left vacant since 1838, and in the course of the next eight years five other members of the pre-1843 Chapter died, the Prebendary of Llanfair in 1845, the Chancellor and the First and Second Canons in 1849 and the Third Canon in 1851. Three vacant stalls were filled in 1851, but their holders were presumably not regarded as members of the Chapter.[48] There remained the Dean, the Archdeacon of Merioneth, the Prebendary of Penmynydd and the Treasurer. The new Archdeacon of Bangor appointed in 1844 claimed membership of the Chapter; the Dean disputed the claim on the ground that the archdeaconry had not yet been annexed to a residentiary canonry and the decision went against the archdeacon.[49]

It was not until 1860 that the new scheme was in operation; the first Canon Residentiary was appointed in that year, and two years later a house was erected to accommodate the canons during their residence. It is doubtful whether much was gained by the new arrangements imposed by Parliament and the Ecclesiastical Commission. It might seem that the cathedral was strengthened by the establishment of the four residentiaries,

[46] P.P. 1836, XXXVI. Fourth Report of Ecclesiastical Commissioners, p. 7.

[47] P.P. 1854, XXV, Cathedral Commission (1852) Report, pp. 87, 565; C.A., Aug. 2, 1853.

[48] In the Clergy List of 1855 they are described as Honorary Canons, a new category allowed under a clause of the 1840 Act which also applied to Wales.

[49] P.P. 1854, XXV, Cathedral Commission (1852) Report, p. 87; C.A. Aug. 2, 1853.

but the system of three-monthly residence was not altogether a success. It was found that the residentiaries had next to nothing to do when in Bangor, while their parishes suffered from their prolonged absence.[50]

The disestablishment of the Welsh church brought with it a diminution of revenue and a change in the arrangements for residence. A new scheme was drawn up in 1920[51] and approved by the Governing Body in 1922, under which instead of the four residentiaries sharing the year between them each member of the Chapter had his period of residence. The Chapter consisted as before of the Dean, the two archdeacons, the two prebendaries, the three dignitaries and the three canons, though in 1930 two further canons, Canonicus Quartus and Canonicus Quintus, were added.

[50] P.P. 1884-5, XXI. Cathedral Commission Report 1885, Bangor, Appendix, pp. 4, 7.
[51] Bangor Cathedral Scheme, 1920. (N.L.W., B/PM/33).

CHAPTER 3

THE CHOIR AND SERVICES

The earliest extant reference to a service in the cathedral is in the account by Giraldus Cambrensis of his tour of Wales in 1188. He describes how the day after the arrival of the party in Bangor mass was celebrated at the high altar by the Archbishop of Canterbury, and Gwion, bishop of Bangor, "on the right side of the altar, overwhelmed by the strong insistence of the archbishop and others, an insistence which had more of importunity than persuasion about it, was compelled to take up the cross, amid much lamentation of his countrymen in the actual church and shouts of grief as well as laments from both sexes accompanied by barbarous cries."[1]

From the fourteenth century we have Dafydd ap Gwilym's reference to the Bangor organ, which, to judge from a poem of Gruffydd Grug addressed to Dafydd, was a recent acquisition.[2] It was perhaps the first organ to be installed. The English cathedrals probably all had organs as early as the mid-twelfth century,[3] but Bangor may well have been as far behind them in the accessories of worship as it was in architectural splendour. In the same century the cathedral obtained an increase of staff. In 1386 the bishop was allowed to appropriate the rectories of Llanynys and Llanfair Dyffryn Clwyd to finance four additional chaplains, who were to pray for the king during his lifetime and the souls of his ancestors and all faithful departed.[4]

Of the arrangements in force in the pre-Reformation period for training the choristers and playing the organ we know nothing. The cathedral music should have been the responsibility of the precentor, but what has been said earlier about the history of the Chapter suggests that this dignitary was introduced relatively late and was of small importance. In 1445 the Chapter handed

---

[1] Giraldus Cambrensis, *Itinerarium Cambriae* II, vi.

[2] *Gwaith Dafydd ap Gwilym*, ed. T. Parry. pp. 42, 396.

[3] Kathleen Edwards, *The English Secular Cathedrals in the Middle Ages* (1949), p. 174.

[4] *C.P.R.* 1385-9, pp. 189-90; Browne Willis, pp. 223-4. The rectory of Llanynys was later annexed to the bishopric, that of Llanfair D.C. to a prebend.

over responsibility for the choral services to the vicars of the parish, who from then on became vicars choral as well as parochial, and probably assumed the direction of the music. The agreement[5] was that in return for this additional duty they should receive "several oblations in the quier, obventions and chorall fees and all the obventions and oblations of Gorvew chapell together with a Garden belonging to that chapell and a house" and the grass of the cathedral churchyard and that of St. Mary's (Llanfair Garth Branan).[6] Though the grant "consisted most in superstitious oblations abolished upon the extirpation of popery, yet by the Deane and Chapter's prevalency with Queene Elizabeth's visitors the said Vicars were injoyned to Quier service as formerly."

The later Middle Ages was a period when numerous chantries were founded with the object of ensuring that prayers were said for the founder's soul. These were sometimes founded for a limited period, sometimes endowed in perpetuity. In the first category comes Bishop Cliderow's foundation of a chaplain to say masses for his soul and perform other duties in the cathedral for a period of five years.[7] In the latter there was Dean Kyffin's chantry of St. Catherine, which in 1504 supported two chantry priests, but in 1535 only one,[8] and that of Maurice Glynn, archdeacon of Bangor, who died in 1525 and founded two chantries in Bangor cathedral and Clynnog church.[9] Cliderow's foundation seems to have survived beyond the five years for which it was intended to last, for it is probably to be identified with the chantry "on an ancient foundation by the bishops of

---

[5] Roger Williams, Vicar and Chancellor, stated in 1690 that he had had a copy of the original agreement, but had given it to his fellow-vicar, Andrew Matthews, and had not seen it again. (N.L.W., B/Misc. Vols./23, p. 153). The quotations given above are from a summary given by Thomas Meredith in a letter to Col. Twisleton of 1657. (N.L.W., B/Misc. Vols./200; copy in B/Misc. Vols./23, p. 223.)

[6] For Capel Gorfew and Llanfair Garth Branan see pp. 101-3. When the former St. Mary's churchyard was incorporated in the bishop's estate, the estate bore a rent charge of 6s. 8d. payable to the vicars. The vicars continued to receive this sum, 3s. 4d. each annually, until the present century, when the land passed into the possession of the University College, and the rent charge was commuted. (Information from Mrs. Garmon Jones.)

[7] Browne Willis, p. 232.

[8] Pryce, *Diocese of Bangor in the Sixteenth Century*, App. A; *Valor Ecclesiasticus* IV, p. 418; *C.P.R.* 1563-6, p. 58.

[9] *C.P.R.* 1548-9, p. 59; 1560-65, p. 592; 1563-8, p. 336.

Bangor" which still existed in 1535.[10] All these foundations came to an end when Henry VIII's Chantries Act of 1545 was carried into effect under Edward VI.

The list of cathedral clergy of 1504 includes one conduct, i.e., hired (*conductus*) or stipendiary chaplain, and the term survived into the seventeenth century. The conducts were then paid £4 each, the sum being met by contributions from the Dean, the Archdeacon of Anglesey and the Prebendary of Llanfair (£2 each) and the Archdeacons of Bangor and Merioneth (£1 each).[11] The full complement was two, but during the episcopate of Lewis Bayly (1616-1631) one of the places was kept vacant, the reason being, according to the Dean, that the bishop, who as Archdeacon of Anglesey was partly responsible for the conduct's salary, refused to fill the place.[12] The conducts, we hear, wore surplices at choir services and sang;[13] under Bishop Bellott (1586-95) one of them used to read the first lesson in English every day at Morning and Evening Prayer, and "did singe the Leateny uppon Wensdaies and Frydaies and all other times when occasions served, at the Quire Doore."[14]

The history of the choir begins with the foundation of the Bangor Grammar School, commonly known as Friars, in 1557. The founder, Geoffrey Glyn, provided in his will for ten poor scholars to receive the sum of £2 annually, and the school statutes directed that they should attend the cathedral wearing surplices on Sundays, holy days and half-holy-days (that is the eves of Sundays and of Saints' days). Whether they were meant to act as choristers was not clear, but as they were there in their surplices it was natural to make them sing. To these foundation scholars, or "Glyn boys" as they were called, were added in 1616 two more boys, recipients of money from another endowment, called "Hutchings boys", though the founder of the scholarships bore the name of Hutchinson.[15] There was also a "Beddgelert

[10] *Valor Ecclesiasticus* IV, p. 418; Browne Willis p. 328. In 1535 the bishop was charged with £6 annually in respect of the chantry, a sum which is more or less the same as the eight marks mentioned in Cliderow's will.

[11] Visitations. Moythe, 1560, J.Griffith, 1632. N.L.W. B/Misc. Vols./23, p. 29.

[12] Visitations. Edmund Griffith, 1623. Cf. Martin, 1617; Griffith, Martin and Mason, 1620.

[13] Visitations. J. Griffith, 1632.

[14] *Ibid.*, Rowland, 1632.

[15] The endowment was transferred from Friars to Botwnog school in the early nineteenth century.

boy", holding a scholarship founded by Maurice Wynn of Gwydir, who is counted among the choristers in the seventeenth-century documents, but by the eighteenth century was no longer required to sing in the choir.[16] In addition there were two choristers proper, who were paid £1 each by the Archdeacon of Merioneth and the Prebendary of Penmynydd.[17]

Under Bishop Rowlands (1598-1616) arrangements were made for the payment of a stipend to an organist;[18] what these arrangements were is not recorded, but it seems likely that, as in the case of the conducts and the two choristers, the stipend was paid by means of contributions from holders of the endowed stalls. We hear of one Thomas Boulton playing the organ and receiving a stipend. But, says Prebendary Griffith in 1632, since the previous bishop, Lewis Bayly, "took the government of all things into his hands", there had been no "constant organist", but continual complaints from Mr. Boulton that his salary was not paid.[19] The author of *The Practice of Piety* does not seem to have been very happy in his dealings with the cathedral; perhaps with his puritan leanings he disapproved of choirs and organs.

The Vicars Choral were considered to be responsible for teaching the boys to sing,[20] but the vicars were not always competent to teach or the boys apt to learn. It is said that the agreement of 1445 laid down that the vicars must be able to sing *cum nota*, but in appointments to the office account was not always taken of musical ability.[21] As for the boys, as Thomas Martin, usher of Friars, put it in 1617, "the children are not sufficiently skilfull in musicke by reason they are not chosen for their voyces."[22] In 1620 however the Dean stated that since the last visitation he had admitted none "without the approbation of one of the vicars for his aptness to sing."[23] John Martin, vicar from 1599, used to teach the boys singing and "their parents did

[16] Visitations. Lewis, Williams, Mason, 1617; Griffith, 1620; Rowland, 1632. Browne Willis, p. 43.

[17] Visitations. Griffith, Martin, Mason, 1620; Griffith, 1632.

[18] *Ibid.*, Rowland, 1632. B/Misc. Vols./23, p. 29.

[19] Visitations. Griffith, 1632. Boulton died in 1644. Browne Willis, p. 37.

[20] Visitations. Moythe, 1560; Mason, 1617; Griffin, 1617; Edmund Griffith, 1620, 1623; Hugh Griffith, 1620.

[21] *Ibid.*, Rowland, 1632.

[22] *Ibid.*, Martin, 1617.

[23] *Ibid.*, Edmund Griffith, 1620.

consider him for his paynes taking with them",[24] and his son Thomas Martin, although not one of the vicars, carried on the work. He stated in 1617 that he "hath taken the paines this twelvemonth and more to teache the singinge boyes, not that he was anie way bound to teach them, but onelye in dutie to his father, and for his own pleasure and practise to further his skill therein. He hath taught one boy perfectly since he began with him foure or five services and about a dozen anthemes or sixteene and hath brought up foure or five more boyes prettily in the skill of musicke, hopinge they will doe well in time."[25]

Soon after the Restoration, as we have seen, a new organ was installed. This was played by one of the Vicars Choral[26] until the revenue from the Llandinam tithes made it possible to appoint a professional organist. In 1690 John Jones wrote: "I conceive that there are many things wanting in and about the church, as particularly the settlement of a Quire and of a good Organist and of Singing men and divers other matters which I hope Llandinam Revenue will by degrees enable us to supply in some good measure and order."[27] The expected improvement began in the following year, when Thomas Roberts was appointed organist at a salary of £14.[28] Evidently he gave satisfaction, for in 1694 his stipend was raised to £18 "in consideration of his care and diligence in his office and place," and in 1698 it was further advanced to £20.[29] He died in 1705,[30] and was succeeded by a Mr. Priest; Bishop Humphreys, now at Hereford, had evidently been asked to help, for the Chapter Order records that Priest was recommended by the Hereford organist.[31] He stayed for only three years, and the next two organists for two and three years respectively.[32] John Rathbone, appointed in 1713, was succeeded by his son Thomas in 1721.[33] The younger Rathbone

[24] *Ibid.*, Rowland, 1632.
[25] *Ibid.*, Martin, 1617.
[26] C.A., Oct. 22, 1689. (Hugh Johnson to be singing man while a vicar choral is organist and no longer.)
[27] N.L.W., B/Misc. Vols./23, p. 33; Pring, p. 151.
[28] C.A., Jan. 27, 1691.
[29] *Ibid.*, May 3, 1694, May 5, 1698.
[30] Browne Willis, p. 37.
[31] C.A., June 14, 1705. He is probably to be identified with the Nathaniel Priest who was later organist of Bristol cathedral. J. E. West, *Cathedral Organists* (1899), p. 7.
[32] C.A., July 14, 1708; Sept. 19, 1710.
[33] *Ibid.*, May 16, 1713; Nov. 22, 1721.

was evidently not an organist of very great ability, for the Dean in answering Visitation questions in 1722 said: "It were to be wished indeed that we had a Revenue to enable us to provide a better Organist and a better teacher of the Choristers."[34]

In 1782 it became possible to raise the organist's stipend to forty guineas, and there were good hopes that the new Green organ would be worthily played when William Shrubsole was appointed at the new salary, with an extra allowance of eight guineas towards the expenses of his journey and the removal of his harpsichord and other effects from London.[35] It was not long before he had to pack up his harpsichord again. Before he came to Bangor he had come under the influence of Edward Perronet, a somewhat extreme Methodist who had broken with Wesley and ministered in an Independent chapel in Canterbury, where Shrubsole was brought up.[36] His religious views soon got him into trouble at Bangor. The Chapter minutes of October 16, 1782, contain the entry:

> Mr. William Shrubsole the organist of this church having given great offence to the Dean and Chapter as well by his close connection with one Abbot of this place as by his frequenting conventicles, Ordered that Mr. Dean be impowered to discharge the said William Shrubsole from his place of Organist if the said Abbot who is supposed to have gone to reside at Dublin should at any time hereafter return in order to abide in the town of Bangor or the Neighbourhood thereof, or if the said William Shrubsole shall be found to frequent any Conventicle or Religious Assembly where any thing is taught which is contrary to the Doctrine of the Church of England.

Evidently Shrubsole did not mend his ways, for in December of the same year he was summoned and given a quarter's notice.[37] His successor was Edmund Olive, who left in 1793,[38] and was succeeded by a relative of his, Joseph Pring, then aged seven-

[34] Pring, p. 152; N.L.W., B/Misc. Vols./23, p. 26.
[35] C.A., Sept. 26, 1782.
[36] Shrubsole's well-known tune Miles Lane, sung to Perronet's hymn "All hail the power of Jesu's Name", was published as early as 1779. See *D.N.B.* under Shrubsole.
[37] C.A., Dec. 24, 1783.
[38] *Ibid.*, Aug. 3, 1784.

teen.[39] Pring was a Londoner and a former chorister of St. Paul's.[40] He took an Oxford doctorate of music in 1808, without residing, as was then the practice with musical degrees. In 1805 he published a volume consisting of twenty anthems composed by himself for the Bangor choir, and at least one of his chants is still in use. He was, as will be seen later, a man of determination, with a high opinion of his own merits and deserts.

The first singing man was appointed in 1689.[41] From 1691 there were two, with a salary of £6, and in 1698 the number was raised to four and the stipend to £8.[42] The number remained unchanged throughout the eighteenth century, as did the stipend, though the latter was raised in 1800 to £10.[43] One of the eighteenth-century singing men, John Lloyd, evidently had a good voice; he received offers from Bristol and Dublin cathedrals, and to encourage him to stay the Chapter allowed him an extra £5, adding, as other bodies have done on similar occasions, that this should not be taken as a precedent.[44] He did stay; perhaps indeed he stayed too long, for when he died in 1752 he was aged 77 and had been a singing man for fifty-nine years.[45] John Lloyd was probably an exception. In Dr. Pring's time at any rate the standard was not high; he complained that unlike those of every other cathedral the Bangor men could not sing by note.[46] Nor were they always regular. In 1753 and 1758 they were admonished for failing to attend practice; in 1789 they were reprimanded for unpunctuality, and in the same year it was noted that they had frequently absented themselves from divine service, and fines were imposed for absence.[47] In 1798 the Chapter Book records the dismissal of one of the men, Thomas Davies, after he had refused to apologise for dis-

---

[39] Pring was appointed by the bishop. His position was regularised when he was formally appointed by the Chapter in 1810. At the same time his salary was raised to £60. Pring, p. 81 n.; C.A., Sept. 28, 1810.

[40] See Grove's Dictionary of Music.

[41] See note 26.

[42] C.A., Jan. 27, 1691; May 5, 1698.

[43] *Ibid.*, Aug. 5, 1800.

[44] *Ibid.*, Jan. 21, 1720.

[45] Pring, p. 76 n.

[46] *Ibid.*, p. 204 n.

[47] C.A., July 11 1753; Sept. 8 1758; Sept. 2 1789; Oct. 1, 1789. On Oct. 20, 1701, it was ordered that "no singing man or singing boy shall either on Sunday or Holyday or Holyday eves wear any Cravatts but onely Bands in Church."

respectful conduct to one of the cathedral clergy; it seems however that the order was not carried into effect, for in 1807 the Chapter dismissed the same Thomas Davies a second time after his conviction for petty larceny.[48] The Chapter did not, of course, record satisfactory attendance and conduct, and a misleading impression may be given by collecting together the occasions on which the singing men were reprimanded. It should be said that in the early nineteenth century, according to Dr. Pring, the choir had as good a record in the matter of regular attendance as that of any other cathedral.[49]

In 1691 it was decided that certain of the Friars scholars who sang in the choir should be constituted "singing boys" and paid from cathedral funds. In that year the following Order was passed:

> That there be four of the present poor boyes or Choristers chosen for singing boyes according to the election of the organist and that their present sallary or allowance be augmented to ffoure pounds a year severally.[50]

In 1698 the salary was raised to £5; the Glyn boys received £2 from their endowment, the Hutchings boys £3 from theirs, so that the former had £3 and the latter £2 from cathedral funds. The four singing boys had the "five pound places", the Glyn boys who were not singing boys had the "two pound places"; all twelve attended the choir services.

Although the singing boys were usually chosen from the Glyn and Hutchings boys, this was not the universal practice. In 1713, for instance, Thomas Rathbone, son of the newly appointed organist, and another boy were elected singing boys. They took the place of two who were demoted to £2 places, and had to wait for vacancies in these before they could be Glyn boys as well as singing boys.[51] The boys who retained their £2 places after their voices broke and they ceased to be singing boys were presumably those who stayed on at the grammar school; others would leave to be apprenticed and vacate their places in the choir altogether.

[48] *Ibid.*, Aug. 11, 1798; March 17, 1807.
[49] Pring, p. 247 n.
[50] C.A., Jan. 27, 1691.
[51] *Ibid.*, Oct. 21, 1713.

The choristers were taught to sing by the organist, sometimes with the assistance of a singing man.[52] Practice was twice a week, on Thursdays and Saturdays, and on one occasion it was found necessary to lay down that this should be in the cathedral and not in a private house.[53] The rest of their education the choristers received in Friars School, where they would pursue the course in Latin and Greek laid down by the Elizabethan statutes. To this course had been added some instruction of a more utilitarian nature, and early in the eighteenth century we find that some of the singing boys were evading their "grammar" and attending the school only for writing and arithmetic. A Chapter Order of 14 July, 1708, reads:

> That whereas divers of the singing boys have of late pretended that they had discharg'd themselves (or by their parents order'd) from learning any more in the Grammar school, and that they attended onely for the sake of the writing school to improve themselves in writing and Arithmetick, it is hereby order'd that from this time forward none shall presume to come to the Free School at Friars upon any such pretence, And that no singing boy shall be capable of receaving the profitts of his singing place unlesse he submitts to be regularly taught in the Grammar place (as the rest are) as well as learn writing and Arithmetick at the proper houres.

That the singing boys did not always attend school regularly is suggested by a Chapter Order of 1795 promoting a boy to a £5 place "provided he give attendance regularly at the grammar school", and by another of 1801 requesting the headmaster of Friars to make a return of those singing boys who regularly attended the school.[54]

In the years immediately following the Restoration the Sunday services were bilingual. Morning and Evening prayer were in English until after the first lesson, when the Vicars Choral left the choir for the body of the church and conducted

---

[52] *Ibid.*, July 21, 1703.

[53] *Ibid.*, Oct. 20, 1701; July 21, 1703; July 23, 1729; June 17, 1748; June 18, 1750. In the order of 1729 a third period, Monday morning, was added. In 1812 there was practice only on Saturday, for one hour before and one hour after evensong. *Ibid.*, Jan. 8, 1812.

[54] *Ibid.*, Nov. 20, 1795; Aug. 11, 1801.

the remainder of the service in Welsh to the parochial congregation. This practice was condemned by Bishop Lloyd in an order of 1684. He observed that "either through the enormous liberties of the late rebellious time or through the connivance of some of the bishops" the service was performed "both irregularly and lamely", the choir service being "but scarce half performed", and ordered that in future the whole service for Morning and Evening Prayer should be said or sung in the choir in English and that on Sundays and Holydays it should also be said in Welsh between eight and ten in the morning and between one and three in the afternoon[55]. This did not please the Vicars Choral, and a few years later they petitioned Bishop Humphreys, claiming that they were not bound to read service more than twice a day. They maintained that the Dean and Chapter had no authority to make laws for the Vicars, that the early morning service (at 6.0 or 7.0 according to the Vicars) was parochial rather than choral and so exempt from Chapter jurisdiction, and that the Prayer Book gave no indication that any service should be read more than once in a day.[56] In spite of this protest the Welsh morning service continued. The duplication of Evening Prayer either was never introduced or was given up; when Browne Willis wrote there was a Welsh service only in the morning.[57]

According to R. Warner in his account of a tour in Wales made in 1797 the bishop had "established a regulation with respect to the service in the cathedral that accommodates both the Welsh and the English by having the offices performed during the forenoon in one language and the afternoon in the other"; and another writer of the same period states that Morning Prayer was in Welsh at 7.0 a.m. and English at 11.0, and Evening Prayer in Welsh in the afternoon.[58] It therefore appears that Welsh evensong was substituted for English, and it is interesting to note that this was apparently done at the instance of Bishop

[55] Pring, pp. 168-9; N.L.W., B/Misc. Vols/23, p. 141.
[56] The petition (original in N.L.W., B/DC/136, copy in B/Misc Vols/23, p. 173) is undated, but is addressed to Humphreys. It does not specifically refer to the Welsh Service, but is presumably connected with Bishop Lloyd's Order.
[57] Browne Willis, p. 31.
[58] R. Warner, *Walk through Wales*, 4th ed., p. 141; J. Evans, *Tour through part of North Wales in the year* 1798, 1800, p. 227.

Warren, who was criticised for his anti-Welsh attitude. For a short period in the early nineteenth century evensong was once more bilingual; but from 1810 evening service was provided in both languages, Welsh at 3.15 and English at 5.0.[59]

The daily said services which were still held when Browne Willis wrote [60] did not survive the eighteenth century; weekday services came to be confined to Wednesdays and Fridays, at one time only when the bishop was in residence, later all the year round.[61] Choral services were on Sundays, holy days and their eves, with two sung services on Sundays and holy days and sung evensong on Saturdays and the eves of holy days. After the establishment of an organist and choir the Chapter made it their business to see that the full cathedral service was sung, with an anthem and a "service" for the canticles. In 1701 it was ordered that there should be an anthem every Sunday (in the morning when the sermon was in English, in the afternoon on the alternate Sundays when it was in Welsh)[62] and that the choir should be allowed till the following Easter to practise for singing the services regularly.[63] According to an Order of 1703 the organist was to have an anthem sung every Sunday, holy day and vigil under penalty of 2/6d.; in 1718 he was required to teach two new anthems every year.[64] It appears that Tallis's was the only service in use until 1703, when three others were introduced, "whereof two at least to be alternate or for both sides."[65] In 1718 Byrd was added to the existing four, and in the same year the organist was required to teach some settings for the Commandments and Nicene Creed.[66]

It is pleasant to be able to record that at the end of the eighteenth century and the beginning of the nineteenth, a period

[59] C.A., Sept. 28, 1810; *N.W.G.* Nov. 15, 1810; Hyde Hall, *Description of Caernarvonshire*, p. 157.

[60] Browne Willis, p. 31.

[61] Pring, p. 22 n.

[62] This arrangement for preaching was altered in 1787 when it was decided to have two sermons a Sunday, one Welsh at the Welsh service and one English at the English. (C.A., Sept. 4, 1787). In 1819 it was decided that the Welsh sermon should be preached by the Vicars, the English by the members of the Chapter in accordance with a new order of preaching. *ibid.*, Nov. 24, 1819.

[63] *ibid.*, Oct. 20, 1701.

[64] *ibid.*, July 21, 1703; Nov. 18, 1718.

[65] *ibid.*, July 21, 1703.

[66] *ibid.*, Nov. 18, 1718. The commandments and creed would be for the ante-communion service, which then followed matins.

when cathedral services were often performed in a perfunctory manner, tourists visiting North Wales were favourably impressed by the Bangor service. According to John Evans, who was in Bangor in 1798, the services were performed "with reverential decorum and a true solemnity of devotion," and fifteen years later Richard Fenton noted "Never did I hear the service performed with more solemnity."[67]

In 1810, with the prospect of a much increased revenue from the Llandinam tithes, the Dean and Chapter considered what to do with the additional sum. They decided to borrow money on the security of their estates for the purpose of building a new parish church for the Welsh congregation, enlarging and improving the accommodation for the choir services and erecting parsonage houses for the vicars.[68] This was in itself a reasonable scheme, but it could hardly be said to come within the terms of the endowment. Building a new church came neither under the heading of repairs to the fabric nor under that of maintenance of the choir. It was therefore necessary to put before Parliament a new bill to amend the Act of 1685. Moreover the scheme had a determined opponent in the person of the organist, Dr. Pring, who took the view that as the endowment was intended in part for the maintenance of the choir, the choir, which he took to mean the organist, singing men and boys, should have their stipends increased.

At the end of November 1811, having heard rumours of the Chapter's new bill, Pring wrote to the Archbishop of Canterbury informing him of the position and asking him to support the choir in their claim for increased salaries. His letter was also signed by the four singing men. One of the four, William Hughes, later abandoned Pring and went over to the other side; the other three supported him throughout.

The application to the Archbishop is explained by certain provisions in the Act of 1685.[69] This stated that the cathedral's share of the Llandinam tithes should be disbursed by the Dean and Chapter "by and with the consent and advice of the

[67] J. Evans, *Tour through Part of North Wales*, p. 226; Fenton, *Tours in Wales*, p. 237.

[68] Pring, p. 33. The plan for building vicarages was later abandoned.

[69] The Act is printed in Browne Willis, pp. 291-6 and Pring, pp. 1-7.

Bishop of Bangor . . . at such rates and proportions as to them shall seem expedient"; any difference between the bishop and the Chapter concerning the application and distribution of the revenue should be settled by the Archbishop of Canterbury. The Act went on to say that if any question should arise concerning the misemployment or non-employment of the revenue, "the same shall and may be heard and determined by the Bishop of Bangor for the time being." The terms of the Act thus left it far from clear whether an appeal should be addressed to the bishop or the archbishop. Dr. Pring held that as the bishop was himself a member of the Chapter through his tenure of the two archdeaconries he could hardly be appealed to from a decision of the Chapter.[70] The archbishop took a different view, and sent a reply consisting of a single sentence; "The Memorial you sent me belongs, I conceive, to the Bishop of your Diocese."[71]

The application to the Archbishop was made without the knowledge of the Dean (Warren), who when he heard of it was not unnaturally annoyed. On December 18 Pring called on him to ask leave of absence to oppose the proposed new bill if it was introduced to Parliament. The Dean willingly agreed, but when he was told of the letter to the Archbishop exclaimed: "Then the choir never shall receive a single farthing of the money while I am Dean of Bangor; for should our intended Act fail, I will take care, that the money shall be so employed, that the choir shall never be benefitted by it."[72] Undeterred Pring proceeded to appeal to the bishop to exercise his visitatorial right and "ward off the impending blow aimed at us", and by so doing to defend "the cause of the oppressed against the oppressors."[73]

The result of this move was that on December 26 Pring was summoned to a Chapter meeting. "Dr. Pring having conducted himself with disrespect to the Dean, the Archdeacon of Merioneth and the Precentor, Ordered that he should be reprimanded and he was reprimanded accordingly." So runs

---

[70] Pring, p. 15.
[71] *ibid.*, p. 11.
[72] *ibid.*, pp. 10 n., 34.
[73] *ibid.*, p. 13.

1. The Cathedral from the South, Eighteenth or Early Nineteenth Century (*from an old print*)

2. The Cathedral from the North-East, Early Nineteenth Century (*from an old print*)

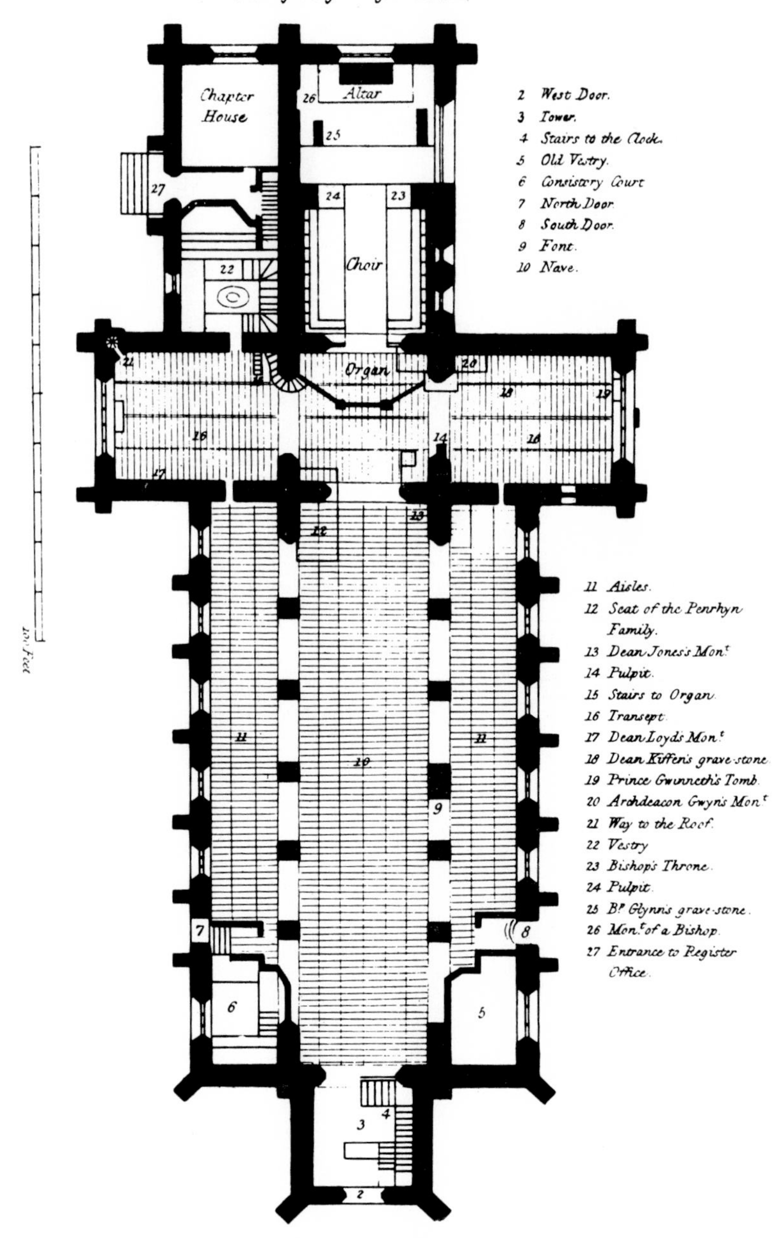

3. Plan of the Cathedral, 1819 (*from Storer's Cathedrals*)

the entry in the Chapter Book.[74] According to Pring the Dean said to him : "Sir, as you appear determined to see that the Chapter do their duty under the Act of King James, we are also determined to screw you up to the utmost of your duty." He had been through the Chapter Books and had found only one order concerning the organist, that he should teach the singing boys the art of singing two hours a week and that for non-attendance he should forfeit 2/6s. "Now Sir, as your salary is three times the amount of what the organist received at that time, we shall increase the forefeit for each non-attendance to 7/6d."[75] On the same day the bishop through his secretary replied to Pring's letter saying that "the Bishop is not aware that the deliberations of the Dean and Chapter have been authoritatively communicated to the Organist and Singing-men, or that any Decree has been actually made and notified by the Chapter to the Complainants, which can afford just ground of complaint, in such form and language."[76] Pring replied in more conciliatory terms, disclaiming any intention of being offensive.

The Chapter was not unanimous, and throughout the dispute the choir had two steadfast supporters in the Treasurer, Thomas Ellis, and the third canon, John Roberts. When in December 1811 a draft of the proposed new Act was circulated to the Chapter for consideration at a meeting on the following January, Pring enlisted the help of these two supporters, and consideration of the draft was deferred for a year.[77] Pring now returned to the charge with the Archbishop, informing him of the state of affairs to date and enclosing copies of his correspondence with the bishop.

Part of the additional moneys had now been received, and at a Chapter meeting on April 1, 1812, it was proposed to make a payment to the two vicars for officiating at the extra Welsh Evening Prayer. J. H. Cotton, the Precentor, had been allotted a guinea a Sunday in respect of the extra duty, though the

---

[74] According to the Chapter's comments on Pring's petition to Chancery, in N.L.W., B/Misc. Vols./23, p. 111, in addition to his disrespectful conduct at the deanery Pring publicly declared that he would not receive the sacrament from the Archdeacon of Merioneth, and insulted the Precentor at the Bishop's Palace.

[75] Pring, p. 183 n.

[76] *ibid.*, p. 14.

[77] *ibid.*, p. 18; C.A., Jan. 8, 1812.

money had as yet not been paid, and when shortly afterwards he became vicar the duty was shared between him and the other vicar.[78] From the pastoral point of view the new arrangement was justified, for the two evening services were better attended that the previous bilingual one.[79] But from the legal point of view it was open to objection, as the new service being parochial should not strictly speaking have been paid for out of cathedral funds. When the question was considered by the Chapter in 1812 there was opposition. Both vicars were members of the Chapter, John Jones as Archdeacon of Merioneth and Cotton as Precentor. As interested parties they properly withdrew when the vote was taken. Four other members were present. The Dean and the Bishop voted in favour of the proposal, the treasurer and the third canon against; the bishop had two votes in virtue of his two archdeaconries and so the proposal was carried. This is the account given by Dr. Pring,[80] who was evidently well informed of what went on in Chapter. His story seems to be confirmed by an addition to the minutes which has been erased and is now illegible. The addition, which presumably recorded the dissentient votes, was erased following an order made at a subsequent meeting, which stated that it had been improperly made while the Chapter was not sitting.[81]

Dean Warren's statement that the choir would get no additional moneys while he was dean was evidently prompted by momentary irritation and did not represent his considered views. In an interview with Pring he expressed the opinion that the Act of 1685 intended a distinct ratio of the Llandinam tithes to be set aside for the maintenance of the choir.[82] Following up this suggestion the choir addressed a memorial to the Chapter for their August meeting of 1812, suggesting the appointment of such a ratio. The meeting however gave no satisfaction to the choir. A draft bill was approved for the building of a new parish church and the alteration of the cathedral; the Bishop, the Dean and the Archdeacon of Merioneth were to form a committee to take the necessary steps to secure the passing of the

[78] Pring, p. 21 n. 35.
[79] N.L.W., B/Misc Vols/23, p. 109.
[80] Pring, p. 22.
[81] C.A., Aug. 3, 1813.
[82] Pring, p. 25.

bill. Certain advances were to be made in the salaries of the choir and officers, except the organist and singing men, who had "conducted themselves in a very disrespectful manner, and more particularly the organist." They were to wait "till such time as by their orderly conduct they shall be esteemed to be equally worthy to receive an advance in their salaries as the other members of the choir."[83] A schedule of new salaries was drawn up which included £80, an increase of £20 on his previous salary, to be paid (eventually) to the organist.[84] The new schedule also included £30 each to the two vicars. Though this proposal aroused the indignation of Dr. Pring, it is only fair to point out that their financial gain was very small if, as appears to be the case, this new payment superseded the guinea a Sunday previously paid to them jointly for the extra Welsh parochial service. Nor would the money they received go into their own pockets, since they now employed a curate,[85] whose salary would probably absorb the £60 allotted to them.

This Chapter meeting was attended by nine members. Three of them, the Treasurer, the Second Canon and the Third Canon, opposed the Order. The Chancellor supported it, but later withdrew his vote. In favour were the Dean, the Bishop, the Archdeacon of Merioneth, the Prebendary of Penmynydd and the Precentor. Dr. Pring points out that three of these were interested parties, the Archdeacon and the Precentor as Vicars Choral and the Bishop as father-in-law of the Precentor.[86] Again there is an addition to the minutes which has been erased.

Pring kept the Archbishop informed of proceedings, and in December was granted an interview at Lambeth Palace.[87] The Archbishop apparently offered his services as arbitrator, but the offer was overtaken by events. The Chapter committee had already resolved to apply for a new Act at the coming Parliamentary session, and Pring decided that he must apply to the Court

---

[83] *ibid.*, p. 28; C.A., Aug. 4, 1812.

[84] When this was communicated to Pring an unfortunate mistake was made; the organist's salary was omitted altogether. Pring, pp. 28, 77, 121 n. The salary is included in the schedule in the Chapter Book, and Pring himself admitted in conversation that he knew this was a mistake. N.L.W., B/Misc Vols/23, pp. 139-40.

[85] Pring, p. 21 n. A curate was appointed in 1810. (Pryce, *Diocese of Bangor during Three Centuries*, p. 52.)

[86] Pring, p. 24.

[87] *ibid.*, p. 29.

of Chancery taking advantage of an Act recently passed "to provide a summary Remedy in Cases of Abuses of Trusts created for charitable purposes." Pring's petition, submitted in January 1813, after recapitulating the case of the choir, prayed that the Chapter Order of August 4, 1812, be rescinded and directions given for the application of the tithes.[88]

The Dean having been served with a notice of the petition summoned a Chapter, and proposed that himself, the Bishop and the Archdeacon of Merioneth be appointed a committee to take such steps as were proper in reply to the petition.[89] The motion was passed by rather dubious means. Only five members were present and three of these, the Treasurer, the Chancellor and the Third Canon, voted against the motion. But the Dean produced three proxy votes, two from the Bishop and one from his brother the absentee prebendary of Llanfair. The Treasurer and the Third Canon formally protested.[90]

The case in Chancery began on April 1, 1813, before Lord Chancellor Eldon.[91] The Counsel for the choir were Sir Samuel Romilly, Mr. Leach and Mr. Bell; on the other side Mr. Hart appeared for the Dean and Chapter and Mr. Richards and Mr. Winn for the Bishop. The first point to be decided was whether the Court had any jurisdiction. The Counsel for the choir argued that neither the Archbishop of Canterbury nor the Bishop of Bangor had visitatorial power applicable to the present case and that therefore such power rested with the Lord Chancellor. The other side maintained that the Court had no jurisdiction. The Act of James II had empowered the Dean and Chapter with the consent of the Bishop to distribute their share of the tithes, and this they had done as they considered appropriate; only if there was fraud or misconduct on their part would the Chancellor have any jurisdiction.[92] The other important point raised concerned the distribution of the tithes.

[88] *ibid.*, pp. 31-37.
[89] C.A., Feb. 16, 1813.
[90] Pring, p. 38. The Chapter Acts confirm Pring's account as regards the supporters of the motion, though there is, as was customary, no record of dissentient votes, nor of a protest. Though Pring throws doubt on the legality of proxy votes, they had, as the Chapter books show, regularly been used.
[91] Pring, pp. 39-105.
[92] This was Hart's argument; Winn for the Bishop submitted that the visitatorial power rested with the Archbishop.

Sir Samuel Romilly maintained that under the Act they were to be distributed according to a settled proportion. For the Chapter it was argued that maintenance of the choir meant providing the persons constituting the choir with such salaries as the Chapter considered appropriate.

The case was by no means a clear one, and Lord Eldon declined to decide until he had studied the Act more fully. In the meantime the Chapter had presented their Bill to the House of Commons, where it had been read a first time. Pring and the three singing men proceeded to submit a petition opposing the bill, which was followed by another from Thomas Ellis and John Roberts.[93] When Pring returned to Bangor after presenting his petition he was summoned to the Deanery, where the Dean read him a series of prepared questions.[94] The first was "Do you disapprove of the Bill?" to which Pring replied "I have read your Bill and disapprove of it *in toto*." The following questions he refused to answer. The Dean prefaced his questions by saying that he conceived it his duty to attend to Dr. Pring's interest, and the intention of the interview appears to have been conciliatory. He also saw the singing men.[95] The three who supported Pring said that they considered themselves bound to act on the advice of Pring's Counsel; William Hughes expressed himself content to confide his interest to the Dean and Chapter. The Dean gave the three men a copy of his conversation with Pring, and added "I trust I have now done my duty to the Chapter, the Organist and the Singing Men. I have endeavoured to prevent what appears to me an unnecessary litigation, originating in misconception and likely to be attended with great and useless expense—I mean the opposition to the Bill now before the House of Commons."

The bill in fact came to nothing. It was given up for the session of 1813 and not brought forward again. In Chancery the Counsel for the choir had admitted, and the Lord Chancellor had confirmed, that there was no reason why the Dean and Chapter should not apply to Parliament for a new bill, but Lord Eldon had pointed out that if Parliament rejected the bill, the

---

[93] Pring, pp. 105-6, 110-113.
[94] *ibid.*, pp. 107-8.
[95] *ibid.*, pp. 108-110.

Chapter could not pay the costs of the application out of cathedral funds. At the annual Chapter in August 1813 it was proposed that the expenses of introducing the bill and of bringing it forward again in the following session should be met by subscriptions from the members of the Chapter who had supported it. The subscriptions agreed on were: £400 from the Bishop (£200 in respect of his two archdeaconries), £200 from the Dean, £50 from the Archdeacon of Merioneth, the two Prebendaries and the Precentor and £10 from the First Canon, "or each subscriber in the like ratio to any amount required."[96] It is not surprising that the bill was abandoned.

The Court of Chancery moved slowly. The Lord Chancellor took over a year to make up his mind on the question of jurisdiction. On May 17, 1814, he announced his decision that this lay with the Chancery Court.[97] Nearly a year later, on April 15 1815, he ordered that one of the Masters of the Court of Chancery, J. S. Harvey, should examine the cathedral accounts and approve a scheme for the application of the tithes; any of the parties concerned were at liberty to lay proposals before the Master, and after he had made his report "such further order shall be made as shall be just."[98] It was not until the end of 1817 that Harvey's report was completed.

The intervening period was occupied with the submission of numerous documents from all the parties concerned. As the endowment was for the repair of the fabric as well as for the choir it was necessary to establish how much was required for repairs. It was in Dr. Pring's interest that the sum should be as small as possible, so that the maximum should be available for the choir. He called in an architect, or builder, John Dale of Maes Incla, Caernarvon, who surveyed the cathedral and concluded that £275 10s. 0d. was sufficient to put it in a state of substantial repair.[99] The Chapter answered this by producing an estimate from John Turner of Whitchurch, Salop, an architect whose views would probably carry greater weight than Dale's. His view was that at least £2,150 was required for repairs; to this he added a further sum for providing increased accommodation for

[96] C.A., Aug. 3, 1813.
[97] Pring, p. 115.
[98] *ibid.*, pp. 129-30.
[99] *ibid.* pp. 156-7

the two congregations, English and Welsh, £2,950 for alterations to the cathedral, with an additional £1,850 for a new church if this was built.[100] Dale having seen Turner's survey revised his estimate, and arrived at the figure of £347 3s. 3d. for repairs, thus proving, according to Pring, that Turner had made a gross overestimate.[101]

The other question was what was meant by "maintenance of the choir". The Vicars Choral had been included in the Chapter's list of claimants on the tithes, and they proceeded to support their claim before the Master.[102] They maintained that they had had an endowment before the Reformation, and that they should have been remunerated under the Act of 1685 and indeed had a better claim than the singing men, as at the time of the Act they and the Chapter were the only members of the choir in existence. On the other side it was pointed out that they were adequately remunerated by the tithes of Bangor parish which they received in virtue of their parochial duty, that they had never been paid out of cathedral revenues since 1685 and that they did not chant but merely read their part of the service.[103] On this point Thomas Ellis and John Roberts deposed that never in their recollection had the Vicars Choral joined in the choral service.[104]

The question was also raised whether the other cathedral clergy should be regarded as members of the choir. The Chapter proposed that the Chancellor, the Precentor and the three Canons should be added to the beneficiaries of the tithes; the Treasurer and the two Prebendaries were presumably omitted because they were already endowed. The Precentor had the strongest claim to inclusion. The usual practice in cathedrals at this time was to leave the direction of the music to the organist and to appoint precentors without regard to their musical ability; but at Bangor it had not been entirely forgotten that the office had something to do with music, and it had from time to time

---

100 *ibid.*, pp. 160-64. In 1812 the Chapter had decided to have the cathedral repaired in accordance with an estimate made by a local surveyor, James Defferd, which was even less than Dale's, £250 13s. 3d. (C.A., Aug. 4, 1812). This decision was not carried out.

101 Pring, pp. 165-6.

102 *ibid.*, pp. 169-171.

103 *ibid.*, pp. 127, 242.

104 *ibid.*, pp. 157-60.

been suggested that the Precentor should exercise his official functions, though without any result,[105] until Cotton was appointed to the post in 1810. The Bishop then told the Dean that he would expect the Precentor to exercise his duties, "in order that the Choral Service might be celebrated in a more correct manner."[106] Cotton was a keen musician, and at once made it his business to superintend the choir,[107] regularly took part in the choral services and attended all the practices. Pring, one may well suppose, did not welcome this interference in what had previously been regarded as his exclusive preserve, and there was evidently some fricton. In January, 1812, when the organist was "screwed up," as the Dean put it, to do his duty, a Chapter Order was passed laying down that the organist "do take all directions relative to the Choir from the Precentor and do submit to the same."[108] In 1815 the Precentor complained of improper conduct and language on the part of the organist "tending to diminish his just Authority and influence over the Choristers"; Pring admitted that his behaviour had been improper and promised not to repeat it.[109]

The Precentor's claim to a share in the income of the endowment gave rise to an affidavit from the Treasurer, who had formerly been Precentor and who deposed that while Precentor he had never sung nor chanted by virtue of his office, nor had he interfered with the musical department of the choir.[110] To this the Dean replied that Ellis's memory had failed him; he had frequently heard him during his tenure of the Precentorship chanting the psalms in the cathedral choir standing in his stall wearing his surplice and hood, which he still did as Treasurer; he had also requested him to exercise his office of Precentor, but Ellis had declined to do so.[111] The present Precentor, Cotton, undoubtedly sang. Whether when he joined in the psalms and

---

[105] *ibid.*, p. 182.

[106] *ibid.* Thomas Ellis claimed that Cotton undertook this work not by virtue of his office but of his own free will (*ibid.*, p. 179), but this seems disproved by the Dean's affidavit quoting Bishop Majendie's remarks.

[107] Cotton said that he gave directions as to what chants, services and anthems were to be performed (*ibid.*, p. 176). Pring said that he himself did this. (*ibid.*, p. 186).

[108] C.A., Jan. 8, 1812; Pring, p. 183.

[109] C.A., Oct. 17, 1815.

[110] Pring, pp. 179-180.

[111] *ibid.*, pp. 181-4.

anthems it was in the capacity of Precentor or as Vicar Choral was a nice point into which he himself did not enter. Pring's comment was: "For one person to produce two distinct voices at the same instant indicates a capacity far beyond what any of our most celebrated ventriloquists have yet attempted."[112]

"It is not easy," in the words of the Dean and Chapter, "to ascertain where to place the Organist."[113] The Counsel for the Chapter argued in the Chancery Court that he was a "superior servant".[114] Pring on the other hand liked to think of himself as an "endowed organist", perhaps the only one in the kingdom, and pointed to a tombstone on which Thomas Roberts, the first organist paid from the Llandinam tithes, was described as "endowed organist".[115] Dean Warren maintained that Pring had no cause for complaint, since he received the salary at which he was appointed.[116] Pring considered his salary "small, and as a maintenance inefficient".[117] It was perhaps small, but it was not, of course, meant as a maintenance. It was expected that the organist would supplement it by giving music lessons, for which the relatively light duties at the cathedral, with no daily services, left ample time. Pring no doubt made a good income as a music teacher; otherwise he would hardly have lived in one of the largest houses in Bangor (Penrallt), sent three sons to Oxford and been able to meet the expenses of his petition to Chancery.[118]

The proposals which he himself put forward would have raised his salary from £60 to £360. When at a later stage in the proceedings the Master proposed to give him four twenty-fourths of the available income, about £106, the Dean and Chapter remarked that if a larger salary than this were given he would be better paid that almost any other organist in the kingdom, and the two Vicars Choral "who are of necessity Gentlemen of liberal and University education" would be placed "in a very degraded situation", adding that "an organist of equal talents might be procured to do the necessary duties for even a less sum

[112] *ibid.*, p. 249 n.
[113] *ibid.*, p. 142.
[114] *ibid.*, p. 73.
[115] *ibid.*, pp. 214, 142 n.; Browne Willis, p. 37.
[116] Pring, p. 188.
[117] *ibid.*, p. 25.
[118] It is said however that the lawsuit so impoverished him that he had to live on credit for some time. West, *Cathedral Organists*, p. 4 n.

than the four twenty-fourth parts."[119] Pring leaves "to the decision of the unprejudiced" whether this comment was dictated "by philanthropic or malevolent minds", and remarks that on the same principle "persons of equal talents might be procured to do the necessary duties (if any) for even a less sum than what the present Dignitaries of most Cathedrals receive."

In addition to his salary as organist Dr. Pring received a small remuneration of ten shillings from each choirboy on admission to a £2 place and £1 on promotion to a £5 place. This was considered to be due to him in his capacity of Master of the Choristers. The Dean and Chapter had hopes of establishing a Master of the Choristers who would not only teach the boys to sing, which was all that Dr. Pring did, but would also have charge of their religious and other education.[120] Such an official seems hardly to have been required, since the choristers received their education in a school of which the Dean and Chapter were governors, and nothing came of the proposal.

The three singing men who had remained faithful to Dr. Pring had nothing to add to what he had to say, but the fourth, William Hughes, sent in an affidavit.[121] Forgetful of the fact that he had expressed himself content to entrust his interests to the Dean and Chapter he made a proposal of his own for distribution which gave more than Pring had proposed to the singing men and boys (he had a son in the choir) and less to the organist. Claims were also made for the singing boys. The parents of the three boys other than Hughes's son thought that Pring's proposals gave too much to the organist and Hughes's gave too much to the organist and men and too little to the boys.[122] Then there was the case of those Glyn scholars who received nothing from the cathedral funds, though they took part in all the choral services and attended practice with the singing boys; their parents submitted that they too were entitled to an increased remuneration,[123] and they had the support of the Dean and Chapter, who proposed to give them £1 each from the tithes.[124] Dr. Pring on the other hand wished to

[119] *ibid.*, pp. 213-4.
[120] *ibid.*, pp. 145, 188-9.
[121] *ibid.*, pp. 202-5.
[122] *ibid.*, pp. 205-6.
[123] *ibid.*, pp. 206-9.
[124] *ibid.*, p. 120. Cf. p. 195.

limit the benefits of the endowment to those members of the choir who had already received emoluments from it. The weakness of his position becomes apparent when we read his comments on the Chapter's proposal to appoint two additional singing men. This very reasonable proposal, which would have given three choirmen, one for each voice, to both sides of the choir, produced the comment: "The Choral Establishment having remained the same for *at least* the last 94 years—can the number of its Members be increased, consistent with justice, at this remote period, by adding *two additional Singing Men*, to the serious detriment of the present Claimants?"[125] On this point the Chapter seems to have had a juster view of the interests of the choir than the organist.

Under the term choir, according to the Dean and Chapter, should be included all persons "deemed necessary for the usual and decent administration of Choral Worship", that is, sacrist, vergers, organ blower, bell ringers, clock winder, cleaner and churchyard minder, the actuary or notary to attend Chapter meetings and a Sub-Treasurer;[126] and as there was no other endowment, it had long been the practice to pay these officials from the Llandinam tithes. Pring had not even included the organ blower in his proposals, although, as the Dean pointed out, an organist was of no use without an organ blower "unless he purposes to play on a barrel or grinding Organ."[127] The organ blower herself, Jane Jones, submitted her claim.[128] She deposed that she had been organ blower for over thirty years, having succeeded her first husband, who had also held the post for about thirty years. She expressed the belief that she had "as great a right to a proportionate share of the distribution as the Organist; for without an Organ Blower the Organist would be quite useless, and the Organ too as it can produce no sound without the working of the bellows." William Williams, the Clock Winder, humbly trusted that the Chancery Court would not only continue his office but advance his salary,[129] though the Lord Chancellor had directed that he could not be regarded as a member of the choir.

[125] *ibid.*, p. 120 n.
[126] *ibid.*, pp. 122-3.
[127] *ibid.*, p. 195.
[128] *ibid.*, pp. 209-10.
[129] *ibid.*, pp. 211-12.

The churchyard keeper had even less claim to be counted as a member of the choir, but he pointed out that but for his efforts considerable damage would be done to the fabric of the church (one of his functions was to stop boys from throwing stones at the windows), and therefore his salary might be considered as coming under the heading of repairs.[130]

On December 24, 1817, the Master made his report. He first outlined the two competing schemes for distribution. These had been somewhat modified as a result of the proceedings and were now as follows. Pring proposed that £275 should be set aside for immediate repairs and £50 per annum for this purpose in the future, and that the residue should be distributed in the proportion of 6/11 to the organist and 1/11 to each of the four singing men, while the remaining 1/11 should be divided between the organ blower and the four singing boys.[131] The Dean and Chapter proposed that the first charge on the increased revenue should be £3000 for repairs. When this sum had been raised, £80 per annum was to be set aside for future repairs and the remainder divided into twenty-nine parts; of these two were to be applied to the expenses of choral services, four were to go to the Precentor and seven to the Vicars Choral, to be divided equally. Nine parts were to be set aside for the organist, Master of Choristers and singing men, among whom the organist was to be reckoned; of this sum the organist was to receive one-fourth, and the remainder was to be divided equally between the Master of Choristers and seven singing men (i.e. six plus the organist). One of the twenty-nine parts was to be shared between sacrists and clock winder, and four between verger, organ blower and six senior choristers; the remaining two parts between the six junior choristers.[132]

The Master's scheme was as follows.[133] He accepted Turner's estimate for repairs, except for the £150 he had included for recasting the bells, and allotted £2000 for this purpose. When this sum had been raised, £60 per annum was allotted to future repairs and the remainder was divided into twenty-four parts. One of those was to go to the expenses of the choral service, four

---

[130] *ibid.*, p. 211.
[131] *ibid.*, pp. 220-21.
[132] *ibid.*, pp. 222-3.
[133] *ibid.*, pp. 223-4.

to the Precentor, five to the Vicars Choral (to be divided equally), five to the organist, six to the singing men (to be divided equally, whether they remained at four or the number was increased); the remaining three, after deduction of the existing wages of the organ blower, were to be divided equally between the singing boys. These proposals satisfied neither party, and each took exception to them.[134] The Dean and Chapter, accepting the sum allotted for repairs and the division of the remainder into twenty-four parts, wished to take two of those parts from the organist and give them to the Vicars Choral, and objected that no provision had been made for the sacrist, the verger, a future Master of Choristers and the churchyard keeper. The exceptions of the choir took the form of a review of their previous arguments and a reiteration of their proposals for distribution.

On August 18, 1818, the Lord Chancellor delivered judgment. "Let the Master appoint a third person to estimate what sum will be sufficient to put the Cathedral in good and substantial repair, and refer it back to the Master to review his Report in this respect. Declare that the Precentor and Vicars Choral are Members of the Choir, within the reach and meaning of the Act of King James II and confirm the Master's report as to the distributions and proportions; and let the proportions given to the Vicars Choral be paid to them as long as they shall do their duties in those characters, and in case of their neglecting so to do, let any person interested be at liberty to apply to the Court."[135] The Chancery case had lasted about five years and still was not finally decided. But subsequent proceedings did not affect the decision. The surveyor appointed by Chancery, Thomas Hardwick, presented his report in March, 1820.[136] He estimated that £1854 was needed for repairs, but the Court allowed the sum of £2000 to stand, so that the Lord Chancellor's judgment of 1818 was in effect final.[137]

Its results were not satisfactory to Dr. Pring. "The Rev. Mr. Cotton," he wrote, "son-in-law to the present Bishop of Bangor, will be the greatest gainer by the new distribution of the funds, for his *six shares and a half*, in his twofold capacity of

[134] *ibid.*, pp. 226-244.
[135] *ibid.*, pp. 245-6.
[136] C.A., April 19, 1820.
[137] *ibid.*, Aug. 4, 1825.

Precentor and Junior Vicar (if the two appointments can be held compatibly by the same person) will produce him about £180 a year, with the hitherto unheard-of advantage of being his *own* Trustee. On the other hand Dr. Pring (who has officiated as Organist 26 years) will be the greatest sufferer by the late Decision; for after having expended in the vain pursuit of impartial Justice, several hundred pounds, to the irreparable loss of a numerous family, his Salary, as Organist, is by the late Decision, a little more than *doubled*, while the salaries of his Colleagues [i.e. the Singing men] have been quadrupled, and the Salaries of the Singing Boys increased to eight times their former amount."[138] Pring had no doubts about the justice of his cause. The documents he published would, he claimed, show "to what unwarrantable expedients Trustees will resort (unless kept in check by the prying eye of those groaning under the galling yoke of oppression) who ought, on the contrary, from the sacred responsibility reposed in them as Guardians, to have imparted to the objects thus placed under their immediate protection a portion of that "brotherly love", which is the hackneyed theme theoretically inculcated by way of precept to others, without evincing, practically, the least semblance of example on their part."[139]

Natural though it is to regard with sympathy those who consider themselves oppressed and claim to fight for justice, it is hard to see Pring as the hero of the story and the Dean and Chapter as the villains. Pring scores some points against Cotton, but we know from other sources that Cotton was not an idle beneficiary of nepotism, but a hardworking clergyman devoted to the interests of the cathedral and parish. His colleagues were able and conscientious men, and at a time when many corporations were forgetful of their obligations, the Bangor Chapter came creditably out of the scrutiny of their affairs which the Chancery case involved. In proposing to amend the Act of 1685 they were attempting to meet the needs of the nineteenth century as the original Act had met those of the seventeenth. They may have been somewhat arrogant in their attitude to their organist, but Pring must have been a difficult man, and his claims on his

138 Pring, pp. 248-9.
139 *ibid.*, p. vi.

own behalf were certainly excessive. It should be remembered that it was not until Pring's appeal to Chancery that any claim was made on the ground that the Precentor and Vicars Choral were members of the choir, and if the law decided that they were, Pring, who had appealed to the law, could not complain. Pring's claims for himself led to counterclaims from others, and what had begun with a disinterested scheme for restoration and new building ended with an undignified scramble for increased stipends on the part of all who could put forward any claims on the endowment.

Dr. Pring continued to occupy the organ loft after the settlement of the Chancery case. His relations with the Chapter cannot have been easy during the dispute, and the book which he published must have been highly displeasing in particular to the cathedral dignitary with whom he had closest relations, the Precentor and Vicar Choral, Cotton. It is to be hoped that indignation on both sides died down, for Pring held his post until his death in 1842.[140] He was succeeded by one of his sons, who had been a chorister and assistant organist, the "kindhearted and painstaking" James Sharpe Pring.[141] It may have been the result of the trouble caused by his father that his appointment was not made for life, but was renewed annually until his death in 1860.

In 1821 the Chapter decided to increase the singing men by two to six, so that alto, tenor and bass should be represented on each side of the choir. At the same time eight of the twelve "surplice boys" (that is, the Glyn and Hutchings boys) were to be selected as choristers, and the other four were to attend services with eight additional boys, making twenty in all; there were to be practices for the boys on holy days and their eves as well as on Saturdays.[142] The decision to appoint two additional singing men brought a protest from the four existing men, whose share of the income would be diminished by the proposal.[143] Whether for this reason or because the Lord Chancellor had not yet confirmed the proposals for distribution, action was postponed until 1826, when an advertisement was issued for counter

140 His tomb can be seen in the cathedral graveyard, near the north door.
141 Hughes, *Recollections*, p. 26.
142 C.A., Aug. 7, 1821.
143 *ibid.*, Oct. 31, 1821.

tenor, tenor and bass (one of the existing men had died meanwhile) at about £50 each and four singing boys at about £18. "The sources," the advertisement added, "from which the salaries arise are rapidly improving."[144] This was an over-optimistic forecast. The tithes, which were let by auction in 1826 for £2155, went for £1995 in the following year,[145] and when they were commuted following the Tithe Act of 1836 the rent charge apportioned was £1615 5s. 0d., of which the cathedral's share was £1076 17s. 0d. But owing to the fluctuations in agricultural prices the actual amount received was often very much less than this.[146] The prospects in 1826 were however sufficiently attractive to tempt men from outside. The vacant places were filled by John McCann of Liverpool, and by Thomas Winterbottom and William Ogden, whose names suggest that they were not local men; and in 1830 John Smith of Lichfield and John Wilkinson of Ashton-under-Lyne were appointed to places which had then become vacant.[147] Instead of appointing the four singing boys for whom they had advertised the Chapter dismissed three of the existing boys and so made vacancies for seven; among the seven elected were two of the Pring family.[148] By 1853 the number of boys had increased from eight to ten and their salary was from £6 to £8.[149] In that year a new scheme was approved by which half the share of the Llandinam revenue originally allotted to the Precentor was assigned to increasing the stipends of the singing men and half to the fabric fund.[150]

The old connection between the choir and Friars school was weakened and finally broken. The Glyn boys continued to sing in the cathedral, but in 1834 only three or four of them were at Friars; the rest received their education at the National school, and although the Friars statutes directed that they should board

---

[144] *N.W.G.*, July 20, 1826.
[145] N.L.W., B/DC/109.
[146] In 1906 the value of the cathedral's share was £738 15s. 1d. gross, £572 16s. 0d. net. Royal Commission on the Church . . in Wales, Minutes of Evidence 46915.
[147] C.A., Oct. 31, 1826; May 6, 1830. Throughout the nineteenth century a certain number of men from outside were appointed to places in the choir.
[148] C.A., Aug. 1, 1826; Oct. 31, 1826.
[149] P.P. 1854, XXV, Cathedral Commission Report, p. 89.
[150] C.A., July 27, 1927.

4. The Interior from the South Aisle, 1818
(from an engraving by H. S. Storer)

5. The Interior from the North Transept, 1818
(from an engraving by H. S. Storer)

6. The Interior of the Choir, *c.* 1840
(engraved by B. Winkles from a drawing by C. Warren)

at the school, they all lived at home.[151] It may be that the education they received at the National School suited them better than the Latin and Greek they would have got at the grammar school, but the Chapter laid themselves open to the charge of misappropriating the endowment and using grammar school funds to pay their choristers. This accusation was in fact made in Parliament in 1844, when W. O. Stanley called attention to a petition presented by Dr. Owen Roberts on the state of Friars school.[152] By this time, it seems, none of the Glyn boys attended the grammar school, and, as Stanley put it, for the sum they received from the charity they were made to sing as choristers.[153]

Services remained as before, except that those on Sunday were by the middle of the nineteenth century somewhat later in the day than they had been at the beginning of the century and English evensong now preceded instead of following that in Welsh. Morning Prayer was at 9.15 in Welsh and 11.30 in English, Evening Prayer in English at 4.15 and Welsh at 6.0. Music of a simple character had now been introduced to the Welsh services, for which there was an unpaid choir in the organ loft, assisted by members of the English choir.[154] This Welsh choir seems to have been rather a disorderly affair; the organ loft, we read, "had become the resort of many drones, not connected with the singing or the cathedral, dropping in at every hour of Divine Service, much to the annoyance and disturbance of the worshippers." Dean Cotton, as he now was, did his best to remedy things by joining the choir at the Welsh morning service, and though he was by then almost completely blind and could not see the offenders, his presence helped to secure good behaviour.[155]

One result of the Ecclesiastical Commission was to bring to an end the old system of choral vicarages. One of the provisions

---

151 Charity Commission Report, p. 486.

152 Hansard, May 23, 1844 (3rd series, LXXIV, 1446-56). According to the report in Hansard the Glyn boys received £2 6s. 0d. The extra six shillings was no doubt due to the increase in the income of the charity noted by the Charity Commissioners in 1834. (Report, p. 486).

153 The cathedral appears to have retained the endowment. In the Cathedral Commission Report of 1885 the return from Bangor includes with the choristers six Glyn scholars at three guineas per annum (Appendix, p. 3).

154 P.P. 1854, XXV, Cathedral Commission Report, App., p. 694.

155 Hughes, *Cotton*, pp. 98-9.

of the Cathedrals Act of 1840 was that cathedral establishments should include at least two minor canons, and the Act of 1843 made no alteration in this respect with regard to the Welsh cathedrals. The peculiar circumstances of Bangor where the existing Vicars Choral also had parochial duties, were apparently ignored. When the bishop in accordance with precedent appointed a new vicar, Evan Pughe, in 1850, it could be maintained that he was ignoring the provisions of the Acts of Parliament since, so far as Pughe's choral vicarage went and if this was regarded as equivalent to a minor canonry, he should have been appointed by the Chapter. Some years later the Chapter disputed his right to hold the post, and in 1860 he was relieved of it, though he was reappointed in 1862. The dispute, which ended with his resignation in 1863, caused some unpleasantness at the time, and some criticism of the Chapter.[156]

The transformation of Vicars Choral into Minor Canons was a lengthy business and entailed much correspondence with the Ecclesiastical Commission. In 1856 the Chapter wrote to the Commission asking for the appointment of Minor Canons and pointing out that when a parish church was built the vicars would be unable to perform their cathedral as well as their parochial duties.[157] Two years later the Commission approved a scheme for the appointment of two Minor Canons in addition to the Vicars, to come into operation as soon as a parish church was built; the Minor Canons were to receive £85 from the Commission, which in addition to the share of the Llandinam tithes which they inherited from the Vicars Choral brought their salaries up to £150, the sum allowed to Minor Canons by the Commission. In the same year one of the vicars died. Though the scheme could not come into operation before the consecration of a parish church or before ratification by Order in Council, the Chapter were allowed to proceed with an appointment.[158] The scheme was ratified by Order in Council in 1860,[159] but it was not until 1865, after the consecration of St. Mary's Church, that the Chapter seal was affixed to the appointment of the two

[156] Hughes, *Cotton*, p. 126, *Recollections*, p. 25; C.A., Aug. 17, 1860; Nov. 20, 1861; Jan. 16, 1862; Oct. 1, 1863.
[157] *ibid.*, June 24, 1856.
[158] *ibid.*, Aug. 3, 1858; Sept. 27, 1858; Oct. 12, 1858. N.L.W. B/DC/61.
[159] N.L.W., B/DC/67.

Minor Canons who had already been in office for a few years.[160]

There was considerable doubt about the duties and status of the Minor Canons. Was their appointment for life? Were they bound to preach? If they did so, should they be paid a fee? These questions were being discussed in Chapter in the eighteen-sixties, but the proposal to submit them to counsel's opinion was not, it seems, carried out.[161] The Chapter evidently regarded the Minor Canons as subject to their orders; in 1873 it was decided that they should officiate at all services, in 1876 that they should attend all full choir practices and in 1885 that they should give religious instruction to the choristers daily.[162] In 1887 a dispute broke out, when the Minor Canons were found to be irregular in attendance and were reminded in writing of previous Chapter decisions. They claimed that they had not been adequately informed of the rules and that they were not bound to attend all services; it was enough to do duty alternate weeks, as the Vicars Choral had done before them.[163] The dispute was submitted to counsel, who gave his opinion that the Minor Canons were a new creation and the precedent of the Vicars Choral was irrelevant. The Dean and Chapter were entitled to make regulations as regards their duties and to make constant attendance at services compulsory; they could not however remove the Minor Canons from office. The bishop, asked to give a decision in the light of counsel's opinion, ruled that express permission from the Dean was required if either Minor Canon wished to absent himself on Sundays, Saints Days or eves, or for several days together.[164]

In 1871 the Chapter appointed, after competition held at the Chapel Royal, a new organist, Roland Rogers, whose career as a church organist began at the age of eleven and ended with his death at the age of eighty.[165] Rogers widened the repertoire and improved the standard. When he came the Te Deum was sung to two chants; by 1892 he had added to the repertoire

---

160 C.A., July 19, 1865; Nov. 28, 1865.

161 *ibid.*, Nov. 17, 1864.

162 *ibid.*, Sept. 10, 1873; Nov. 14, 1876; Oct. 17, 1885.

163 *ibid.*, July 1, Aug, 10, 1887.

164 *ibid.*, March 22, 1888.

165 *ibid.*, June 20, 1871. Robert Roberts, who succeeded J. S. Pring in 1868, died after three years at the age of thirty.

thirty services and three hundred anthems.[166] He had however some disagreements with the Chapter. In 1880 he was asked to resign, but allowed to withdraw his resignation on certain conditions.[167] In 1891 he was informed that the Dean disapproved of his conducting musical performances in nonconformist chapels and he proceeded to resign. An attempt was made to patch up the dispute, but in January, 1892 the Chapter passed an Order: "Inasmuch as it is most important to the good order of the cathedral that the relations between the Dean and the Organist should be of a friendly character and inasmuch as there is no prospect of the restoration between them of such relations, ordered that we accept with great regret the resignation of Dr. Rogers."[168] The break with Rogers was not however final and irrevocable; in 1906 when his successor, T. Westlake Morgan, resigned, he was reappointed, and he is commemorated by a tablet in the cathedral.

In the last quarter of the nineteenth century the cathedral was more ambitious in the matter of choral services than either before or later. In addition to the existing services a daily choral evensong was introduced during the summer months.[169] The choir evidently thought themselves overworked and underpaid; in 1899 the Minor Canons, Organist and lay clerks (this more dignified term was now preferred to the old "singing men") addressed a memorial to the Dean and Chapter raising a number of points with regard to their status and emoluments and asking whether either their stipends could be increased or their duties lessened by either discontinuing the daily choral service in summer or by allowing the two sides of the choir (decani and cantoris) to attend alternately. The Chapter answered in the negative,[170] but a few years later, in 1902, the Ecclesiastical Commission agreed to take over responsibility for the whole of the Minor Canons' salaries; this released the money they had previously received from the Llandinam tithes,

---

[166] P. B. Ironside-Bax, *The Cathedral Church of Bangor* (1907), p. 54. There is a very unfavourable account by John Addington Symonds of the singing in 1861, under J. S. Pring. H. F. Brown, *John Addington Symonds, A Biography* p. 112.

[167] C.A., June 21, Aug. 3, 1880.

[168] *ibid.*, Dec. 3, Dec. 8, 1891; Jan. 13, Jan. 27, 1892.

[169] In 1892 the months of choral daily service were May to September, in 1915 June to September. See the Bangor Diocesan Calendar for those years.

[170] C.A., Oct. 26, 1899.

which was applied to raising the salaries of the choir and organist.[171] On the disestablishment of the Welsh Church the Llandinam endowment, since it had been acquired after 1662, escaped secularisation and was transferred to the Representative Body for the use of the cathedral. It continued to be applied to the purposes laid down in the Act of 1685 as interpreted by the Chancery Court.

The twentieth century has seen an inevitable lightening of the burden of the choir. The daily sung service in the summer has gradually faded out, as have the two sung services on saints days and the one on their eves. Today the choral service is normally confined to Sundays and one weekday evensong. Changed social conditions have made it impossible to maintain it on the old scale; today a vacant lay clerkship no longer attracts applications from distant towns and a choristership is no longer a sought-after "place". The choral service however still continues, though on a reduced scale, and the modern successors of the old Glyn boys are still, in Thomas Martin's words, "brought up prettily in the skill of musicke".

[171] *ibid.*, Nov. 3, 1902.

CHAPTER 4

THE OFFICE OF SACRIST

In 1348 Iorwerth Vychan and Elidir ap Madoc are recorded as holding free of charge two messuages and six bovates of land in return for serving in the cathedral and looking after the service books.[1] The land they held was at Tyllvaen, in what is now known as Glanadda. Their duties and their property descended to a single sacrist in the post-reformation period.[2]

In the early nineteenth century, at the time of the Pring case, the office was held by William Hughes, who was also parish clerk. He stated that he received rent from a tenement and two small quillets in the parish; the Dean and Chapter however described his property as a considerable farm.[3] His duties were chanting the psalms and making the responses, taking care of the communion plate and linen, looking after the books belonging to the choir, locking the choir doors, seeing that the bell was rung at the proper time and giving notice of choir service.[4] His "chanting" was described by Pring as "bawling the melody of the chant eight tones and a half below the choristers", and was put an end to.[5]

In 1883 the sacrist let some of his land on an eighty-year building lease.[6] The rest of his property he sold, and invested the proceeds in consols. In 1906 he received £105 per annum interest on his investment and £35 in ground rent.[7] His duties were to attend all services, look after the books connected with the services and take care of the communion vessels,[8] in fact very much what Iorwerth Vychan and Elidir ap Madoc did in

---

1 *Record of Caernarvon*, p. 94.

2 See N.L.W., B/Misc. Vols/23, p. 160.

3 Pring, pp. 201, 121. He was also paid £3 19s. 0d. per annum from the Llandinam tithes.

4 Pring, p. 201.

5 *ibid.* The sacrist was evidently a different man from the William Hughes who was a singing man at the time.

6 C.A., June 24, 1884.

7 Royal Commission on the Church of England . . in Wales and Monmouthshire Report, 1911, Minutes of Evidence 46915.

8 *ibid.*, 46917.

the fourteenth century. After Disestablishment the endowment was transferred to the Representative Body for the use of the Dean and Chapter.

CHAPTER 5

THE LIBRARY[1]

Only one of the service books which belonged to the cathedral in the Middle Ages is in its possession today. Bishop Anian's Pontifical[2] was written in all probability for the first Bishop Anian in the later thirteenth century; it came into the possession of Bishop Ednam, who gave it to the cathedral in 1485. At the beginning of the eighteenth century it was in the hands of Bishop Humphreys, by whom it was once again presented to the cathedral. Other service books which the cathedral acquired by will or otherwise, such as the missal and ordinal bequeathed by William Loring in 1414 and the pontifical left by Bishop Cliderow in 1435, have been lost.[3]

A bequest which shows the influence of new ideas in religion was made by Bishop Bulkeley in 1552. He left three Bibles, two English and one Latin, and directed that an English and a Latin bible were to be placed in the choir and the other English bible in the "cross Ile", that is the parochial part of the church.[4] These bibles perhaps disappeared under the Marian regime. At any rate the visitation returns of 1560 and 1567 record that there was only one English bible, and that torn.[5]

Bishop Bulkeley was also responsible for establishing a cathedral library in the proper sense, to provide reading matter for the clergy. In his will he bequeathed a number of books "to be delivered when the said library be erected and set up and not before."[6] This library building, which was apparently an independent structure on the south side of the cathedral, was erected presumably soon after Bulkeley's death, but was taken down by 1617.[7] It is described by one of the canons, J. Griffith,

---

1 For a history of the cathedral library see the introduction, by Maura Tallon, to the catalogue by E. Gwynne Jones and J. R. V. Johnston.

2 For a full account of Anian's Pontifical see T. J. Morris in *T.A.A.S.*, 1962, pp. 55-85.

3 For Loring's bequest see p. 43, n. 20; for Cliderow's Browne Willis, p. 232.

4 *ibid.*, p. 257.

5 Visitations. Myrian, William Powell, Moythe, Maurice Powell, 1560; Evans, Bulkeley, 1567.

6 Browne Willis, p. 257.

7 Visitations. Lewis, 1617.

in 1632. "There stood a library by the south doore of the cathedral church which was an ornament unto the church in my opinion and very useful for strangers and prebendaries that came to preache: there was in it an upper and a lower roome. In the upper room there was a chimney for fire, convenient seates, with ledges for books and formes to sitt uppon." It was evidently not well supervised. Griffith goes on to say: "I never was in it but once with Mr. Hill, for I heard that it was once well stored with books and that most of them were taken away thence, and lest I should be taxed among other with purloyning of any, I did forbear to go unto it."[8] This building disappeared leaving no trace, and there is no mention of it in any printed account of the cathedral.

The next we hear of the cathedral books is in 1699, when the Chancellor of the Cathedral stated that he had seen in the vestry or chapter house twelve folio books in Latin which he took to belong to the church; he had himself borrowed two and the rest had been borrowed by another person and apparently not returned.[9] In the eighteenth century, as we have seen, a library was constructed on the north of the choir. In 1722 the Dean reported: "We have a library room belonging to the church but not quite finished. We have no books as yet, except a lending library. But the bishop of Meath [John Evans, formerly bishop of Bangor] has promised divers times in open Chapter to bestow his library upon this church and I hear he has lately expressed himself to the same effect."[10] Whether the bishop of Meath carried out his promise does not appear to be recorded; the library, as we have seen already, was first fitted up to receive the books left by Dean John Jones on his death in 1727.

The lending library referred to was installed in 1710. It was provided by the S.P.C.K. under Dr. Bray's scheme for establishing parochial and diocesan lending libraries, and according to Browne Willis, consisted of "a good number of valuable books

[8] *ibid.* Griffith, 1632.

[9] N.L.W., B/Misc Vols/23, p. 154.

[10] *ibid.*, p. 27 (also in B/VSR/25) Cf. Browne Willis, pp. 19-20. At this time there were also two books, Hammond's Paraphrase of the New Testament and the works of Baxter, presented by a former Vicar of Conway, Mr. Morgan, kept chained on a desk in the north transept. Bodleian MS Jesus College, 115, p. 47.

chiefly in divinity, which are kept in two handsome presses."[11]

The cathedral library received important accessions in the nineteenth century as a result of gifts by H. Longeville Jones, Henry Barber and Hugh Beaver Roberts, and in 1950 when the Canonry was sold the more valuable books from its library were transferred to the cathedral.

In 1960 the library was deposited in the University College of North Wales, where it is kept as a separate unit in the College library. The catalogue produced by the College in 1961 replaces that compiled by C. W. F. Jones, Minor Canon and Cathedral Librarian, in 1872. The library as it now is consists of some 4,500 volumes, including four incunabula.

---

[11] Browne Willis, p. 20.

CHAPTER 6

EPISCOPAL AND OTHER RESIDENCES

When Archbishop Baldwin visited Bangor in 1188 he and his party were, as Giraldus Cambrensis tells us, "decently entertained" by the bishop, Gwion.[1] The bishop must then have had a fairly substantial residence in the city, but no trace of it survives, nor is anything known of any other palace in Bangor earlier than that erected at the end of the fifteenth century. In the intervening period the bishop when in the diocese presumably resided elsewhere, in particular on his manor at Gogarth, where the ruins of an episcopal palace can still be seen. This is believed to have been erected at the end of the thirteenth century by the first bishop Anian, and was probably burnt at the beginning of the fifteenth century in the course of Glyndŵr's rebellion.[2]

The palace in Bangor was begun by Bishop Deane and completed by Bishop Skevington.[3] It appears to have originally consisted of a great hall on a (roughly) east to west axis, with a wing projecting to the south and service rooms to the east of the hall; somewhat later another wing projecting south was added at the east end. The building was timber framed, and by the mid-seventeenth century was much decayed.[4]

Considerable alterations and improvements were made in the eighteenth and early nineteenth centuries. The palace as it was in 1721, after it had been improved by Bishop John Evans, is described by Browne Willis. The entrance was through an arch by the stables, over which were granaries. On the ground floor was a large hall, a wainscoted parlour and a servants' hall, a kitchen, laundry and other offices, On the first floor was a consecrated oratory, a handsome dining room and bedrooms.[5]

---

1 Giraldus Cambrensis, *Itinerarium Cambriae* II, vi.

2 See R.C.A.M., Caerns Inventory I, p. 113, where there is a full architectural description of the surviving remains.

3 So Humphrey Humphreys in Wood, *Athenae Oxonienses* II, col. 742. An inscription over the entrance (Browne Willis, p. 41) read "Thomas Skevington ep's Bangor fecit"; but Humphreys's statement that it was begun by Deane deserves respect.

4 See R.C.A.M., Caerns Inventory II, pp. 9-10, III, p. 115.

5 Browne Willis, p. 41.

A new stairway on the north was constructed in 1753, during the episcopate of Zachary Pearce, and further improvements were made by Bishop Warren, who was probably responsible for the elegant plaster ceiling in the drawing room, now the Council Chamber. According to a writer of 1792, "the present worthy bishop, Dr. J. Warren, a person of taste and genius in improvements, has laid out large sums of money upon the premises and made them convenient and comfortable. His Lordship for five or six months in the year keeps a seat of hospitality, and entertains the ladies, gentry and clergy of his diocese at his festive board, with plenty and elegance and with the plaintive melody of the harp."[6]

In 1809 H. W. Majendie was translated to Bangor. As he had thirteen children it is not surprising that he needed more accommodation. He added the extension to the north which, as is recorded on a slate tablet, was erected in 1810. His initials (H.B. for Henricus Bangoriensis) can also be seen over the arch erected in 1812, which was formerly the entrance to the palace grounds and now leads to the cathedral garden. Richard Fenton describes the palace as it was when he visited it in 1813 after Majendie's improvements. It had had "a great deal laid out on it by the present Bishop, most judiciously and with great taste, so that a more charming residence cannot be. The Hall, which everyone remembers a dark, funereal room, by opening new windows to the Park, made light and cheerful, serving as an excellent family breakfast room, and also for a chapel for family prayers. The Chairs happily designed, being stained black, the backs wrought with Gothic pinnacles, and the openings Gothick with a gilt Mitre in raised work on the centre of the back. Cane bottoms. Drawing room very handsome, lighted by one handsome Venetian window opening on a balcony under a Verenda to the Lawn of the Park, with a pleasing side view of the Cathedral, and the surrounding hills prettily fringed with wood."[7]

The "charming residence" described by Fenton did not satisfy Watkin Williams, who was appointed to the bishopric in 1899, and though one can hardly agree with his view that the

[6] [Nicholas Owen], *Caernarvonshire, A Sketch of its History . . .*, 1792, p. 53.
[7] Fenton. *Tours in Wales*, p. 237.

house had no antiquarian interest, it must be admitted that the unculverted Adda which ran in front of it and was liable to overflow, must have detracted from its amenity.[8] The bishop moved to a house at Glyngarth on the Menai Straits, and the old palace became the Town Hall. The Glyngarth palace was given up by the next bishop, Daniel Davies, and a house on the road between Bangor and Menai Bridge became the episcopal residence until Bishop J. C. Jones moved back to Anglesey, to a house beyond Menai Bridge on the road to Llanfairpwll. The final move was made by Bishop G. O. Williams. In 1963 a new Bishop's house was built in Bangor, from the designs of Messrs. Pinckney and Gott of London.

The present Deanery dates in part from the 1680's, when a new house was built by Humphrey Humphreys to replace one which in 1623 was described as "in sufficient repair",[9] but by 1649 was "ruinous".[10] Humphreys's house was enlarged and largely rebuilt in 1863, the architect being G. P. Benmore of Bangor.[11] In 1956 it was divided into two, and now houses the canonry as well as the deanery.

In the seventeenth century the three archdeacons and the Treasurer each held small plots of land in Bangor.[12] These may be assumed to have been the sites of former houses attached to their offices. One of these houses, that of the Archdeacon of Bangor, was, if we can believe the tradition perpetuated by Shakespeare, the scene of the meeting between Owain Glyndŵr, Hotspur and Mortimer at which they divided the kingdom between themselves. These houses disappeared at an unknown date, and there were no capitular residences other than the deanery until 1862, when a substantial Gothic house was built for the benefit of the residentiary canons. This house was sold to the University College in 1950, and the ground floor is now used as an art gallery.

In 1445 when the vicars took over cathedral duty they were given a house by Dean John Martyn, which was known as Plas Martyn, the upper rooms being allotted to the senior vicar

---

[8] N.L.W., B/OC/84.
[9] Visitations, Brynkir, 1623.
[10] Browne Willis, p. 283.
[11] N.L.W., B/DC/123.
[12] Browne Willis, pp. 284-7.

and the lower to the junior.[13] In 1632 one of the vicars stated that it was not in good repair, "yet for all that but a little wants which we will repayre,"[14] but not long afterwards the vicars refused to live in it "because it had neither garden nor backside nor any externall conveniency lefte."[15] It became ruinous and was leased to the deputy registrar to convert into a stable "and other useful buildings."[16] The house still existed in 1810 when Fenton observed in the High Street opposite to the cathedral "the facade of an old building entered by a pointed Arch Doorway,with a small window of ancient stone tracery on each side,"[17] which he understood to have been formerly the vicars' residence. After this building had been abandoned there was no vicarage until 1815 when the senior vicar, John Jones, built one, the present "Old Vicarage", at the east end of the churchyard.[18] This continued in occupation until 1910 when the bishop purchased it from the vicars and gave it to the Dean and Chapter to be used for diocesan societies and meetings.[19] A large room for meetings was then added; further enlargements and alterations were made in 1965.

---

13 N.L.W., B/Misc/200; B/Misc Vols/23, p. 32.

14 Visitations, Rowland, 1632.

15 N.L.W., B/Misc/200.

16 N.L.W., B/Misc Vols/23, p. 149.

17 Fenton, *Tours in Wales*, p. 212. The site, Mrs. Garmon Jones informs me, was that of Albion Buildings (now occupied by Timpson's shop and John Pritchard's Office.)

18 C.A., Feb. 27, 1815. According to Hughes, *Recollections*, p. 49, the vicarage was built by Hamer, vicar from 1819.

19 C.A., Sept. 1, 1910.

CHAPTER 7

FRIARS SCHOOL

The Bangor Grammar School (Friars), though the Dean and Chapter were its governing body, was not strictly speaking a cathedral school, in that it was an independent foundation and not, as were the "King's Schools" of the former monastic cathedrals, an integral part of the cathedral establishment; nor was it a choir school, though its scholars served as choristers. But in view of the connection which it had with the cathedral for more than three hundred years of its history some account of it must be included here. This need only be brief, since the history of the school has been recorded elsewhere,[1] and its relation to the cathedral choir has been dealt with in an earlier chapter of this work.

The school's founder, Geoffrey Glyn, an Anglesey man, brother of William Glyn the Marian bishop of Bangor, acquired in 1553 the lands and buildings of the suppressed Bangor Friary, and died in 1557 leaving this property and an additional endowment for the foundation of a grammar school. Letters Patent issued in 1561 made the Dean and Chapter its governing body, and statutes were approved in 1568. These statutes, which were closely modelled on those of Bury St. Edmunds grammar school (founded in 1550), gave, as was usual at the time, precise directions for the conduct of the school and its scheme of studies. It was a five-form school, the first three forms being taught by the usher and the fourth and fifth by the master. The curriculum, which is similar to that of other grammar schools of the period, comprised a course in Latin beginning in the first form with the rudiments and ending in the fifth with the reading of Virgil, Cicero, Caesar and Sallust; the Greek alphabet was learnt in the third form in preparation for beginning on the grammar in the fourth.

The school continued to be housed in the old Friary buildings until the end of the eighteenth century, when it moved into new

---

[1] Barber and Lewis, *History of Friars School*, 1900; *The Dominican*, Fourth Centenary Number, 1957.

premises. Bishop Warren, whatever his other misdeeds, served Bangor well as regards its grammar school. He took a personal interest in its fortunes, and was the moving spirit in providing it with new buildings. It was he too, in all probability, who brought to Bangor from Oxford an able Welshman, Peter Williams, to serve as headmaster on the school's re-opening in 1790. For the next forty years or so the school flourished; then it began to decline, until in 1867 it closed altogether. Other old grammar schools experienced a similar decline at a time when the classical curriculum which they were required by statute to offer no longer met the needs of the day; but at Bangor the process was accentuated by the appointment in 1838 of an unsuitable headmaster, W. C. Totton, who remained in office until his death in 1867. In 1873 the school re-opened under Daniel Lewis Lloyd, later bishop of Bangor, but in that year a new scheme came into operation under which the Dean and Chapter ceased to be the governing body. The subsequent history of the school does not therefore concern us here.

Photograph by Geoffrey Charles

7. The Choir and Sanctuary

8. The Mostyn Christ

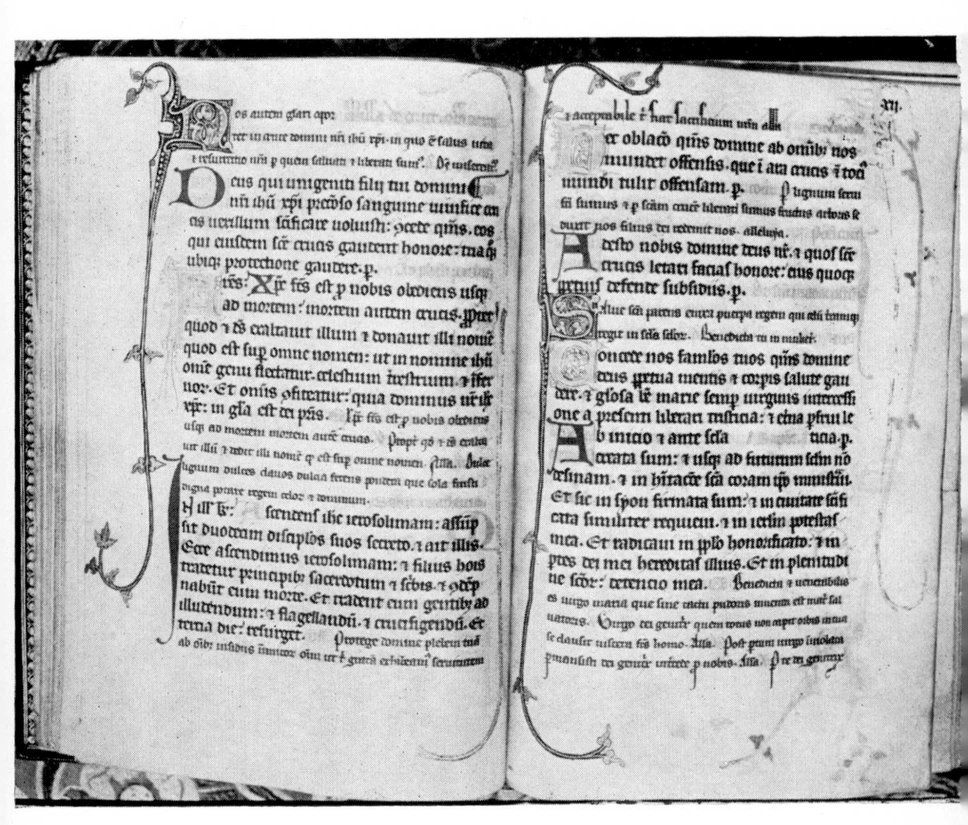

9. Bishop Anian's Pontifical

CHAPTER 8

BISHOP HENRY ROWLANDS CHARITY

This charity[1] was founded by Bishop Rowlands under his will dated July 1, 1616. He left property in the parish of Llansadwrn, Anglesey, to maintain "six poor almsmen, old and impotent, of honest name and fame." They were to be unmarried men, from the parishes of Penmynydd, Aberdaron, Mellteyrn, Bangor, Llangristiolus and Amlwch, and were to receive two shillings a week maintenance and "six yards of good white frieze apiece to make them gowns towards winter, every year." They were required to attend divine service in the cathedral on Wednesdays, Fridays and Sundays.

They were allotted a house in Bangor formerly occupied by the Registrar, George Steel. This was replaced in 1805 by the present almshouses, built on a different site, on the south side of the cathedral, at a cost of £650. In 1774 the allowance was raised to four shillings a week and a matron was appointed at a salary of two shillings a week. Increases in the revenue of the charity made it possible to raise these sums further, and by the end of the nineteenth century the almsmen and the matron received nine shillings a week each. Each of the men had two rooms, and the matron had a bedroom and a kitchen on the premises.

In 1958 it was decided to modernise the premises so as to provide four bed-sitting rooms with separate bathrooms and kitchens on the ground floor and two flats on the first floor. The plans were drawn up by Messrs. North and Padmore and the total cost was £8,341 1s. 11d. The renovated almshouses were opened in October, 1960, by the Minister for Housing and Local Government, Henry Brooke.

A new scheme for the foundation was approved by the Charity Commissioners which allows the flats to be occupied by married men and for one of them to be let to a matron or warden;

---

[1] I am grateful to the Revd. Evan J. Jones, secretary to the Trustees, for providing me with the material for this section. I have added a few details from the reports of the Charity Commissioners.

contributions from the tenants are permitted, and applicants may be accepted from parishes other than those named in Bishop Rowlands's will.

CHAPTER 9

BANGOR PARISH AND CHURCHES

Before 1888 Bangor was a large single parish including Pentir and other hamlets as well as the town of Bangor. Pentir, otherwise known as Llangedol, was originally a separate parish, and is mentioned in 1284, when its vicar acknowledged the receipt of twenty shillings as compensation for damage sustained by his church in the wars of Edward I.[1] The benefice was apparently appropriated to the priory of Beddgelert[2] until at an unknown date it was united with Bangor, and a system established under which two vicars shared the tithes and the parochial duties with, from 1445, the additional responsiblity of conducting the cathedral services.

In the episcopal registers of 1521 Hugh Holland is described as presented to one of the perpetual vicarages in the cathedral "cum rectoria ecclesie parochialis Sancti Cedoll unita et annexa" and the Valor Ecclesiasticus (1535) records that the vicars choral share the rectory of Llangedol, value £17 . 0 . 2.[3] It would appear that this sum includes the emoluments of Bangor parish, as these are not otherwise mentioned and at a later date the vicars undoubtedly shared the tithes of the whole parish, rectorial and vicarial.[4] The fact that they were always known as vicars rather than rectors was probably due to their vicarial status in the cathedral. Bangor parish was thus, in technical

---

[1] *Litere Wallie*, p. 67, No. 113.

[2] See *Caernarvonshire Historical Society Transactions*, 1960, map opposite p. 16. In the Valor Ecclesiasticus we have the paradoxical situation that, though the rectory of Pentir was then annexed to the choral vicarages of Bangor, it appears, as chapelry or vicarage, without any value attached to it, among the benefices belonging to Beddgelert. (*Valor* VI, pp. xvi, xviii). Lewis's Topographical Dictionary, under Bangor, states that the parishes of Bangor and Pentir were united before 1402, when Pentir was taken by the Abbot of Valle Crucis, who restored it in 1444 when the parishes were re-united. Perhaps Valle Crucis is a mistake for Vallis Beatae Mariae (Beddgelert), but I have been unable to discover any authority for the dates given. If 1444 is correct, it could be connected with the assumption by the vicars of choral duties in the following year.

[3] A. I. Pryce, *The Diocese of Bangor in the Sixteenth Century*, p. 4; *Valor Ecclesiasticus* IV, p. 418, VI, p. xxiv.

[4] In the mid-seventeenth century the benefice of Pentir alone was said to be worth not more than £10 (N.L.W., B/Misc/200).

terms, a consolidated comportionate vicarage[5]; this arrangement continued into the nineteenth century and its last relics were only abolished in 1937.

As we have seen earlier, the Chapter's hopes of using the Llandinam revenue to build a parish church in Bangor in 1810 were frustrated. By the middle of the nineteenth century additional accommodation was badly needed, especially in the summer months when the town was filled with visitors. In 1857 it was said that thousands had had to stay away from the cathedral owing to lack of room and that churchmen had been compelled to attend English services in dissenting chapels.[6] In that year money had already been subscribed and sites given for two new churches, but it was not until 1864 that St. Mary's was consecrated, followed in 1866 by St. James's. The parish however remained a single one, though in 1864 the vicars agreed to divide it into districts, one of them being responsible for lower Bangor and St. Mary's, the other for Upper Bangor and St. James's, with the Welsh services at the cathedral; the duty at Pentir was shared between the two.[7]

In 1888 Pentir was detached from Bangor and became a separate parish, and in the same year the new parish of Glanadda (St. David's) was formed. What remained continued as a single parish with two vicars, and at one time the practice was for the senior of the two to take charge of St. James's and the junior of St. Mary's. In 1937 two separate parishes were formed, the cathedral precincts being left as extra-parochial.[8] In 1955 the vicarage of St. James was united with the deanery of the cathedral, but this arrangement was terminated in 1962.

A Charity School was established in Bangor about 1710,[9] and Dean John Jones on his death in 1727 bequeathed the sum of £100 for the education of ten poor children.[10] By the 1830's

[5] So Lewis's Topographical Dictionary. Lewis's statement that the parishes of Bangor and Pentir were re-united in 1657 after being separated at the Reformation must be wrong. A. I. Pryce's *Diocese of Bangor in the Sixteenth Century* records no presentations to Pentir separately. It seems that what happened in 1657 was that Thomas Meredith, vicar of Bangor, attempted to unit the two vicarages into one (See N.L.W. B/Misc/200). If this was done, it was soon undone at the Restoration.

[6] *N.W.C.*, Sept. 12, 1857.

[7] N.L.W., B/Misc/137

[8] N.L.W., B/Misc/129.

[9] *T.A.A.S.*, 1952, p. 40.

[10] *ibid.*, p. 41. Charity Commission Report 1834, pp. 487-8;.

this charity had almost outlived its usefulness. A schoolmistress was then employed for £5 a year, but her pupils numbered only five girls and two boys; as the Charity Commissioners observed, "this small number of children proceeds from the increased opportunities afforded at the National and Infant Schools."[11] The National School had been opened in 1822; it was situated in Dean Street on land leased from the Dean and was erected at a cost of £600.[12] It was replaced in 1868 by a new school in Garth Road, designed by Kennedy and O'Donoghue.[13] Schools were erected at Pentir in 1814 and at Vaynol in 1816; the latter was replaced by a new school in 1859.[14] The Upper Bangor school (Cae Top) dates from 1872.

A new graveyard was opened in 1840;[15] it was converted to a public garden in 1951. The cemetery at Glanadda was opened in 1862; its chapel, the foundation stone of which was laid in 1857, was designed by W. Morris of Oswestry.[16]

Llanfair Garth Branan

The old parish church of St. Mary (Llanfair Garth Branan[17]) stood on rising ground to the north of the cathedral in what is now College Park.[18] Its exact site has not been established. It has been suggested that the foundations discovered in the park in 1925 are those of the church, but they appear to belong to a building too small and rude for the parish church of a place as important as Bangor.[19]

---

11 *ibid.*

12 For a description of the opening ceremony see Hughes, *Cotton*, pp. 18-22.

13 *N.W.C.*, Feb. 15, 1868.

14 Hughes, *Cotton*, p. 15.

15 Hughes, *Recollections*, p. 51.

16 *N.W.C.*, May 30, 1857.

17 Called "ecclesia Sanctae Mariae de Garth Branan" in a note in Bp. Anian's Pontifical (Browne Willis, p. 72); "Garth Branan" in Visitations, Mason 1617; "Garth Branant" in N.L.W., B/Misc/200; "Erw Fair" in B/Misc/Vols/23, p. 149. "Llanfair Erw Nant", used in Hughes and North, *Old Churches*, p. 195 and R. C. A. M., Caerns Inventory II, p. 12, appears to have no authority.

18 Browne Willis, p. 46, states that the church was about four hundred yards from the cathedral. This would be almost at the top of the hill, which seems an unlikely site. There were no traces of the church when Willis wrote.

19 *Arch. Camb.* 1925, p. 435; Archaeology in Wales, News Letter of Group 2 of British Council of Archaeology, Report by L. Alcock of excavations undertaken in 1964.

It is recorded[20] that in the church there was an inscribed stone stating that its founder was the Saxon king Edgar (tenth century); but as another inscription gave Athelstan, who was earlier than Edgar, as one of its benefactors, these claims cannot be regarded with complete confidence. In 1291, according to a note in Bishop Anian's Pontifical, Anian held a synod of the clergy of the diocese in the church.[21] The church is referred to as if still standing in 1486/7;[22] one might surmise that it was abandoned after the rebuilding of the cathedral nave by Bishop Skevington, though it may have remained in use until 1540, when a building described as "Our Lady Chapel in Bangor" or "the Church of Bangor" was demolished and the material used for royal works at Caernarvon.[23]

CAPEL GORFEW[24]

This was a small chapel to the east of the cathedral on the site of the former Diocesan Registry in what is now Ffordd Gwynedd.[25] It is said to have been a chapel of the Hospitallers of St. John.[26] It was in use in 1445 when the vicars of the parish were granted the oblations in the chapel in part return for their

---

20 Browne Willis, p. 183.

21 *ibid.*, p. 72. Browne Willis (p. 80) deduced from a commission issued to Robert, Bishop of Lamburgh, in 1371 during the vacancy of the see of Bangor, that the church had recently been rebuilt. The words of the commission, "ad dedicandum et reconciliandum quascunque ecclesias parochiales civitatis et diocesis Bangorensis dedicatione seu reconciliatione indigentes" (Reg. Wittlesey, Lambeth Palace Library) do not bear out this deduction.

22 ". . . unum gardinium in Garth Vranan jacentem inter coemiterium quoddam ecclesiae Stae Mariae Virginis in praedicta Garth Vranan et horreum Magistri Ric. Kyffin." Quoted by Henry Rowlands in a letter of 1719. Bodleian MS Jesus College 115, p. 124.

23 See the accounts published in *Y Cymmrodor* XXVII (1917), pp. 83 f. These are difficult to interpret. One would naturally take the words quoted above to refer to the former parish church of St. Mary, but references to carrying stones from "the Friars of Bangor" to the water side, evidently part of the same operation as the demolition of the church, suggest that the church or chapel in question belonged to the Friary, which was then in the possession of the Crown. See Glyn Roberts in *The Dominican* 1927, p. 20.

24 Ecclesia Scti Gwrvyw, 1586/7 (Penrhyn rental quoted Bodleian MS Jesus College, 115, p. 129); Gorvew chapel, 1657 (N.L.W., B/Misc/200); Gorfriw, 1685 (N.L.W. B/Misc Vols/23, p. 49f); Goethroy, 1690 (*ibid.*, p. 149).

25 I am grateful to Mrs. Garmon Jones for help in identifying the site of the chapel. The land attached to it included the now derelict garden opposite the Old Vicarage in Waterloo Street.

26 *Arch. Camb.* 1846, pp. 241-2. No evidence is given for the statement.

undertaking the cathedral duties.[27] After the Reformation it became a barn. At one time it was in the hands of the bishop, but it was recovered by the vicars and served as a tithe barn. About 1815 it was taken down and the site sold.[28]

St. Mary

The second St. Mary's church, consecrated in 1864, was built at a cost of £4,650, to which Col. E. G. Douglas Pennant, later Lord Penrhyn, contributed £2,000. It was designed by H. P. Horner of Liverpool.[29] It is in the Decorated style and consists of chancel, nave and aisles of six bays, with arcades without capitals and clerestorey of small trefoil windows. At the east end of the south aisle is a tower with octagonal belfry stage and spire. The organ dates from 1899. In 1958 the church was renovated at a cost of about £8,000.

The church house dates from 1929. It was designed by Richard Hall of Bangor and erected at a cost of about £3,500.

Eglwys y Groes, Maesgeirchen

This church, on a new housing estate in the parish of St. Mary's, was consecrated in 1958. The architect was S. Colwyn Foulkes of Colwyn Bay. The cost of site, building and furnishing was £16,600.

St. James

This church[30] was designed by Kennedy and Rogers of Bangor and built at a cost of nearly £6,000;[31] the foundation stone was laid in 1864 and the church consecrated in 1866. It was regarded as a memorial to Dean Cotton, who before his death in 1862 had collected £1,400 towards its erection.[32] It is in the Decorated style, and originally consisted of chancel, nave with north aisle and tower with spire over a south porch (north and

---

[27] See p. 53.

[28] N.L.W., B/Misc/200; B/Misc/Vol/23, p. 49f., p. 149f.; *Arch. Camb.*, 1846, pp. 241-2.

[29] *Church Builder*, 1865; *N.W.C.* Oct. 29, 1864. See also the extracts from documents published in a centenary pamphlet, 1964 (pages unnumbered).

[30] See P. A. Mainstone, *The Church and Parish of St. James, Bangor*, 1955.

[31] Hughes, *Cotton*, p. 154; £4000 according to Williams' *Sixpenny Guide to Bangor* (1896), p. 87.

[32] Hughes, *Cotton*, p. 154.

south are here used in their ritual sense; the church is not orientated). A south aisle was added in 1884; in this the windows and buttresses of the original south wall were re-used.[33] In 1894-5 new vestries and organ chamber were added and new choir stalls erected, from the designs of Arthur Baker and Harold Hughes.[34] The pulpit dates from 1905 and a new entrance from the vestry from 1925. The original organ was replaced by a new one in 1895, which was modernised in 1952-3. In 1965-6 alterations were made to the interior arrangements, involving the moving of the organ from the organ chamber to the west end of the south aisle and of the choir stalls to the eastern part of the nave.

PENTIR, ST. CEDOL

Scanty remains of the old church can be seen in the churchyard to the north of the present church. The wall running north and south of which the lower part remains seems to have been the east wall of a structure consisting of nave and chancel with a south chapel whose east wall was on a line with that of the chancel.[35] The dimensions of the church can be roughly gauged from the dates of the gravestones, since, apart from the slabs belonging to interior burials, stones earlier than 1848, when the new church was completed, must have been outside the old church. This evidence points to a building about fifty feet long, the width at the east, including the chapel, being about thirty feet.

Prebendary John Ellis, writing to Browne Willis in 1719, states that the church was built by the family of Plas Pentir and was still repaired by them, in return for which they claimed the right of burial throughout it.[36] The reference is probably to the rebuilding said to have taken place in 1694,[37] which however was

---

[33] *Byegones relating to Wales* 1884-5, p. 112.

[34] N.L.W., B/F/38.

[35] In R.C.A.M. Caerns Inventory II, p. 242, it is pointed out that the wall appears too thin to be part of any substantial medieval building. The Commission do not say more than that "it may be associated with the earlier church", but it is hard to see what else it could have been than the wall of the church.

[36] Bodleian MS Jesus College 115, p. 40. In 1710 Thomas Williams of Ty-yn-y-ffrith bequeathed an annual rent-charge of ten shillings for the repair of the church. His will is transcribed in BM Add MSS 32644.

[37] Hughes and North, *Old Churches*, p. 205. No source is given for the statement.

perhaps only partial, since it involved the retention of what looks like a late medieval ground plan. When the Williams family of Plas Pentir died out there was doubt as to who was responsible for the repair of the church, and it was "in a very dilapidated state" before it was repaired in 1817.[38] By the 1840's it was again in a sad state. " I have seldom seen," wrote a parishioner, "a more neglected interior in any church in Wales. The windows are patched and broken, the cloth partly covering the Altar table mildewed and tattered and the rest of the church in keeping with this forlorn condition."[39] A tablet in the new church gives the seating capacity of the old one as 190. It must have been well filled with pews and benches and these evidently extended to a point very near the communion table. Among the brass tablets transferred to the new church is one recording that Anne Greene lies buried "between the pews underneath"; Anne Greene's gravestone remains *in situ* very near to where the communion table must have stood.

The new church, which was consecrated in 1848, was designed by Henry Kennedy.[40] It is in the Early English style, and consists of nave and chancel, with vestry and south porch and a double bell gable at the west. The chancel arch is supported on corbels and there is a stone pulpit entered by a doorway from the vestry. The fittings, apart from the former Communion Table of 1702, are contemporary with the building.

GLASINFRYN, ST. ELIZABETH

This church dates from 1871 and was designed by Sir Gilbert Scott, who presented the plans.[41] It was enlarged in 1897 by an extension to the west and the addition of a porch and organ chamber (which is still awaiting the intended organ). The architect of the additions was P. Shearson Gregory.[42]

---

[38] *N.W.G.*, Dec. 11, 1817.

[39] *N.W.C.*, April 7, 1846. The Sunday service was then at the inconvenient hour of 1 p.m., when most of the parishioners would normally be having dinner, as the curate had to hurry to Bangor for the afternoon service at the Cathedral.

[40] Foundation stone laid May 27, 1847; consecration Aug. 10, 1848. *N.W.C.*, May 25, 1847, Aug. 15, 1848.

[41] *The Builder* 1871, p. 773.

[42] *N.W.C.*, Nov. 6, 1897.

RHIWLAS, ST. GEORGE

Built in 1897 from the designs of John Williams of Llandegai.[43]

ST. DAVID, GLANADDA

The church was built in 1888 at the expense of Mrs. Elizabeth Atcherley Symes as a memorial to Dean H. T. Edwards; the architect was Sir Arthur Blomfield.[44] It consists of nave, transepts and chancel, with south chapel and organ chamber on the north of the choir; there is a tower at the south-west, containing a peal of eight bells. The windows are mainly single or grouped lancets; in the aisles there are cinquefoil windows over pairs of lancets. The exterior is of local stone with dressings of Ruabon stone; for the interior facing red brick is used. The low iron screen dates from 1936 and the Lady Chapel altar from 1937. A new organ was installed in 1907.

ST. PETER, PENRHOSGARNEDD

An iron structure erected in 1878 was replaced in 1956-7 by the present church, in a simplified Gothic style, designed by P. M. Padmore.

[43] *N.W.C.*, May 15, 1897.
[44] *The Builder*, 1888, p. 354.

APPENDIX I

Lists of Bishops, Cathedral Dignitaries, Canons, Vicars Choral, Minor Canons, Organists and Vicars of the Parishes

These lists have been compiled with the aid of the following works; Browne Willis, *Survey of the Cathedral Church of Bangor*; Le Neve, *Fasti Ecclesiae Anglicanae* 1300-1541, XI, The Welsh Dioceses, compiled by B. Jones, 1965; A. I. Pryce, *The Diocese of Bangor in the Sixteenth Century* and *The Diocese of Bangor during Three Centuries*; Crockford's Clerical Directory ; R. R. Hughes, *Biographical Epitome of Bangor Clergy* (typescript in U.C.N.W. library). Additions to these sources are indicated by footnotes. Dr. J. W. James has kindly supplied me with notes on the pre-Norman bishops.

In the case of the cathedral Chapter it is not possible to establish the successions to the various stalls further back than the sixteenth century. I have therefore, except in the case of the Deans and Archdeacons, included all dignitaries, canons and prebendaries up to 1541 in a single list, though in some cases towards the end of that period it is known what stall they held. For the period before 1541 the date of presentation is indicated thus: 1425-; that of death or cession thus: -1425; the date at which the person in question is known to have been in occupation of the stall thus : (1425). After 1541, since the successions are, with a few exceptions, established, only the date of presentation is normally given.

BISHOPS

Deiniol *c.* 546-584
Elfodd (Elbodug) *c.* 768-809[1]
Morlais -944
Dyfan *c.* 1055-
Revedun *c.* 1081-
Hervé 1092-1109
David 1120-1139
Meurig 1140-1161
Gwion (Guy, Guido) 1177-1190
Alan 1195-1196
Robert of Shrewsbury 1197-1213
Cadwgan (or Martin) 1215-1236
Richard 1237-1267
Einion (Anian) 1267-1307
Gruffudd ab Iorwerth 1307-1309
Einion (Anian) Sais 1309-1328
Matthew de Englefield 1328-1357
Thomas de Ringstede 1357-1366
Gervase de Castro 1366-1370
Hywel ap Goronwy 1371-1372
John Gilbert 1372-1375
John Swaffham 1376-1398
Richard Young 1398-1404
Llewellyn Bifort (Byford) 1404-1408
Benedict Nicholls 1408-1417[2]
William Barrowe 1418-1423
John Clederowe (Cliderow) 1423-1435
Thomas Cheriton 1436-1447
John Stanbury 1448-1453
James Blakedon 1453-1464
Richard Edenham (Ednam) 1465-1494
Henry Deane 1494-1500
Thomas Pigot 1500-1504
John Penny 1505-1508
Thomas Skevington 1509-1533
John Salcote (or Capon) 1533-1539
John Birde 1539-1541
Arthur Bulkeley 1541-1553
William Glyn 1555-1558
Rowland Meyrick 1559-1566[3]
Nicholas Robinson 1566-1585
Hugh Bellott 1586-1595
Richard Vaughan 1596-1597
Henry Rowlands 1598-1616
Lewis Bayly 1616-1631
David Dolben 1632-1633
Edmund Griffith 1634-1637
William Roberts 1637-1665
Robert Morgan 1666-1673
Humphrey Lloyd 1673-1689
Humphrey Humphreys 1689-1701
John Evans 1702-1715
Benjamin Hoadley 1716-1721
Richard Reynolds 1721-1723
William Baker 1723-1727
Thomas Sherlock 1728-1734
Charles Cecil 1734-1737
Thomas Herring 1738-1743
Matthew Hutton 1743-1747
Zachary Pearce 1747-1756
John Egerton 1756-1768
John Ewer 1769-1774
John Moore 1775-1783
John Warren 1783-1800
William Cleaver 1800-1806
John Randolph 1807-1809
Henry William Majendie 1809-1830
Christopher Bethell 1830-1859
James Colquhoun Campbell 1859-1890

[1] "Archiepiscopus in guenedote regione". *Annales Cambriae* (*Y Cymmrodor* IX, p. 163)
[2] Appointed by Gregory XII. Griffin le Yonge, appointed in 1407 by Benedict XIII, the rival pope at Avignon, did not take possession of the see.
[3] Morys Clynnog was appointed in 1558, but not consecrated.

Daniel Lewis Lloyd 1890-1899
Watkin Herbert Williams 1899-1925
Daniel Davies 1925-1928
Charles Alfred Howell Green 1928-1944
David Edwardes Davies 1944-1949
John Charles Jones 1949-1957
Gwilym Owen Williams 1957-

DEANS

(1162) Arthur de Bardsey
(1236) Guy[4]
(1254) William[5]
(1286) Kyndelw
(1291) William
(1328) Adam
-1371 Hywel ap Goronwy
(1371) (1382) John Martyn[6]
1389- Walter de Swaffham
(1396) William Clyve[7]
(1397) David Daron
-1410 William Pollard
1410-1413 Henry Honore
1413-1416 Roger Wodele
(1423) (1436) Nigel Bondeby
(1445) John Martyn
(1464) Hugh Alcock
(1468) Huw Morgan
(1480)-1502 Richard Cyffin
(1502) David Yale
1503- Richard Cowland
(1509)-1534 John Glynn
1534-1554 Robert Evans
1554 Rhys Powell
1557 Robert Evans[8]
1570 Roland Thomas
1588-1593 Held by the bishop in commendam
1593 Henry Rowlands
1599 Richard Parry
1605 John Williams
1613 Edmund Griffith
1634 Griffith Williams
1672 William Lloyd
1680 Humphrey Humphreys
1689 John Jones
1727 Peter Maurice
1750 Hugh Hughes
1753 Thomas Lloyd
1793 John Warren
1838 James Henry Cotton
1862 James Vincent Vincent
1876 Henry Thomas Edwards
1884 Evan Lewis
1902 John Pryce
1903 Griffith Roberts
1934 Henry Lewis James
1940 Thomas Alfred Williams
1941 John Thomas Davies
1955 John Richards Richards
1957 Hywel Islwyn Davies
1962 Gwynfryn Richards

---

[4] *C.P.R.*, 1232-1247, p. 149.
[5] *Valuation of Norwich* (ed. W. E. Lunt), p. 194.
[6] John (1371) presumed identical with John Martyn (1382).
[7] On Nov. 17, 1396, William Clyve effected an exchange with Philip Clyffield of the deanery for the vicarage of Woolaston, Glos., but as the reverse exchange took place on May 24, 1397, Clyffield has not been included in the list of deans. *Register of John Trefnant* (Canterbury and York Society, 1916), p. 190.
[8] Reinstated, having been ejected in 1554.

ARCHDEACONS OF BANGOR

(*c*. 1132) Maurice
(1145)-1151 Simon
(1157) David
(1166) (1188) Alexander
(1248) (1263) David[9]
(1284) K-[10]
(1291) Caducan
(1324) Griffin Trefor[11]
(1328) William
(1345) Ithel ap Cynwrig
(1345) Elias
(1367) (1391) Gervase ap Madog
(1394) (1396) Robert de Higham
-1399 Iorwerth ap Madog
1398- Walter de Swaffham
-1412 John de Carnyn[12]
(1411) (1417) Thomas ap Rhys
(1431)-1433 Thomas Banastre
1433- John Heygate
(1436) Thomas Banastre
(1453) (1468) John Parsons[13]
(1504)-1525 Maurice Glynne
1525-1556 Thomas Runcorn[14]
1556 Edward Gregory
c. 1560 Edmund Meyrick
1606 Edmund Griffith
1613 Richard Gwynn
1617 Edward Hughes
1633 William Mostyn
1669-1685 Held by the bishop in commendam
1685-1844 Annexed to the bishopric

ARCHDEACONS OF ANGLESEY

-1236 Richard
-1268 Anian
(1283) (1286) Madog ap Kenrick
(1287) Gruffydd ap Madog Fychan
(1301) Madog ap Tudur
-1309 Anian Sais
(1317) Anian
(1324) Madog ap Meurig
(1328) Madog Hedwich
(1345) John
-1368 Hywel ap Goronwy
1368-1395 Thomas Harborough
1395-1398 John ap Rhys
-1398 Walter de Swaffham
(1405) Evan ap Bleddyn
-1410 Thomas Hywel
1410-1413 John Wolde
1413- Thomas Hywel
(1428) (1440) Andrew Holes
(1446) (1452) William Saundir
(1469) William Moggys
(1504)-1524 Richard Bulkeley
1524-1537 William Glynn
1537-1554 John Salisbury
1554 George Griffith
1558 Griffith Roberts
1559 John Salisbury[15]
1573-1584 Held by the bishop in commendam
1583 Owen Owens
1592-1685 Held by the bishop in commendam
1685-1844 Annexed to the bishopric

---

[9] *Littere Wallie*, pp. 77, 111.
[10] *ibid.*, p. 82. Perhaps the same as the following.
[11] *C.P.L.*, II, p. 241.
[12] *ibid.*, VI, p. 251.
[13] *Register of John Stanbury* (Canterbury and York Society), p. 6.
[14] Runcorn is almost certainly the unnamed person recorded as presented in 1525.
[15] Reinstated, after having been deprived in 1554.

ARCHDEACONS OF BANGOR AND ANGLESEY

1844 John Jones
1863 John Wynne Jones
1887 John Pryce
1902 John Morgan
1921 Albert Owen Evans
1937 Henry John Morgan
1947 Richard Hughes
1957 Gwynfryn Richards
1962 Evan Gilbert Wright

ARCHDEACONS OF MERIONETH

(1328) (1331) Tudur ap Adda
(1358) Tudur ap Dafydd
(1377) (1387) Samuel de Wyk
1387- John Sloleye
-1404 John ap Rhys
1404- William Fychan
(1405) Griffin le Yonge
-1410 Matthew Peyworden (alias Wotton)
1410- Roger Hungarten
1416- John Estcourt
(1436) Richard Gele
(1485) Richard Bulkeley
(1504) (1513) Richard Bromfield
-1524 William Glynn
1524-1562 William Roberts
1562 Nicholas Robinson
1574 Humphrey Robinson
1576 Edmund Prys
1623 Robert White
1660 Robert Morgan
1666 John Lloyd
1668 William Lloyd
1672 Simon Lloyd
1676 Michael Hughes
1681 Hugh Pugh
1683 Francis Lloyd
1712 Lancelot Bulkeley
1716 Richard Langford
1733 Hugh Wynn
1754 John Ellis
1785 John Roberts
1802 Peter Williams
1809 John Jones
1834 Richard Newcome
1857 Henry Weir White
1866 John Evans
1891 Thomas Williams
1906 John Lloyd Jones
1931 Thomas Alfred Williams
1940 David Jenkins
1953 Henry Williams
1959 Walis Huw Thomas

CANONS AND PREBENDARIES TO 1541

(1267) Gervase[16]
(1284) Grigorius[17]
(1291) Madog[18]
(1291) David[18]
(1291) Caducan[18]
(1291) Elias[18]
(1291) Griffin[18]
(1304) Hugh de Leminster
-1308 Walter Reynolds
-1309 William de Melton
1309- Ralph de Melton[19]
(1309) Gregory ab Einion
(1309) Matthew de Neuyn
(1309) Thomas de Cauntebreg

[16] *C.P.R.*, 1266-72, p. 165.
[17] *Litere Wallie*, p. 66.
[18] *Taxatio P. Nicholai*, p. 290.
[19] *C.P.R.* 1307-1313, p. 176.

(1317) Adam de Murimuth
1318- Dafydd de Rudulbach
(1324) Madog ap Meurig
(1328) Einion ap Meurig
(1328)
Matthew de Archllechwedd
(1328) Einion ap Tegwareth
(1328) John ap Gruffudd
(1328) Dafydd de Guellt
(1328) Dafydd de Rhuddallt
-1328 Matthew de Englefeld
(1330) Madog Ddu
(1330) David Philippi
1330-1340 Thomas Fastolf
(1343) John de Dyffrynclwyt
1343-1346 John Trefor
1344-1351 Robert de Tresk
1347- Edmund Trefor
1351- Hugh de Monyngton
(1349)-1352
Peter de Gildesburgh[20]
1352- Peter de Wotton [21]
-1355 Robert Pollard
-1358 Madog ap Dafydd Llwyd
(1357)-1402 Ithel ap Robert
1358-(1361) John Gruffudd Ddu
1361- Robert de Shardlowe
(1363)-1415 William Loryng
1363- Thomas Howe
(1366) Ralph de Ringstede
(1366) Thomas Delves
-1375 Thomas de Lynton
1375-1380 John de Carleton
1380-1409 William
de Humblestane
(1387)-1395 William Seman
1387- John Bentley[22]
-1389 Griffin Tresgoet
1389- John de Burton
1390- Hywel ap Madog
1395- Nicholas Stoke
-1398 Ieuan ap Dafydd Fychan
1398-1410 Gruffudd Trefor
-1398 Lewis Aber
1398 Richard Prentys
1398- Robert Egerley
-1399 Thomas de Lenia
1399- Thomas Martyn
-1400 Thomas Llyn
(1400) (1404) Griffin le Yonge
1402 Thomas de Everdoun
1402- John ap Goronwy Goch
(1405) William Fychan
(1404)-1409 John Wotton
1409- William
1410- John Brampton
1410-1417 Thomas Knight
-1413 Thomas Hywel
1414- Thomas West
1415- Nicholas Julian
1417-1422 Edmund Nicholls
(1422) Thomas Faukes
1422-1444 William Ryley
(1423) John Dalton
(1423)(1450) John Graystock
1424- John Pye
-1424 John Tylton, senior
1424- John Tylton, junior
(1430) Hugh Alcock
(1440) Robert Appulby
(1441) Huw Tregar
(1446) William Saundir
(1464) William Conwey
(1482) Ralph Heithcote
(1504) John Gregger (Precentor)
(1504) (1509) Huw Elis (Chancellor)
(1504) (1509) Richard Fychan (Prebendary of Llanfair)
(1504)-1518 Richard Bangor (Treasurer)
(1509) Richard Grygg (Canonicus Tertius)

---

[20] *C.P.L.* III, p. 314, *C.P.R.* 1350-1354, p. 212.
[21] *ibid.*
[22] Seman is recorded as having exchanged his prebend with Bentley in 1387 (*C.P.R.* 1385-1389, p. 353), but also with Stoke in 1395.

(1509) Richard Myrion (Prebendary of Penmynydd)
(1509)-1517 Robert Pyldeston (Canonicus Primus)
(1509) Dafydd Trefor (Canonicus Secundus)
(1509)-1530 David Yale
(1504)-1520 Thomas Ireland (Precentor)
1517- Dafydd ap Gruffudd (Canonicus Primus)
1518- Thomas David
1520- Dafydd Gruffudd
1530-1541 William Knight
(1534)-1541 Arthur Bulkeley
(1534) William Cleyburgh
(1534)-1554 Huw ap Robert (Canonicus Tertius)
(1534) (1535) John Huws (Chancellor)
(1534) (1535) John Huws or ap Hywel[23]
(1534) (1535) Dafydd Llwyd (Prebendary of Penmynydd)
(1534)-1554 Lewis Newburgh (Treasurer)
(1534) (1535) John Robyns (Precentor)
(1535)-1550 William Capon (Prebendary of Llanfair)
(1535) (1541) Dafydd ap Madoc[24]
(1539) (1541) Huw Goch
(1541) Lewis ap Tudur

PREBENDARIES OF LLANFAIR[25]

1550 John Gwyn
1551 Griffith Gwyn
1555 John Gwyn[26]
1575 Richard Gwyn
1617 John Baylie
1619 John Roberts
1626 William Hill
1660 John Jones
1668-1673 Held by the bishop
1673 Simon Lloyd
1676-1679 Held by the bishop
1679 Francis Lloyd
1713 John Ellis
1735 John Conant
1779 Richard Evans
1797 Henry Warren
1845-1856 Vacant
1856 John Jones
1877 Evan Lewis (Canon Residentiary)
1884 John Pryce (Canon Residentiary)
1888 Thomas Jones
1889 Daniel Evans
1892 Daniel Silvan Evans
1897 Evan Thomas Davies
1906 David Jones
1910 John Price Lewis

---

23 Perhaps identical with the previous John Huws.
24 Perhaps identical with Dafydd Llwyd, Prebendary of Penmynydd. The episcopal registers record the resignation in 1554 of Davld Lloyd ap Madoc from the Prebend of Penmynydd.
25 Browne Willis gives the following successions to the prebend: David Yale (-1520 (*sic*)); William Knight (1520(*sic*)-1541); Fulk Salisbury (1541-1543); William Capon (1543-1550). On the other hand according to the Valor Ecclesiasticus William Capon held the prebend in 1535 and there is no mentions of Salisbury's collation in Bulkeley's register (the first entry dates from March, 1541; no register is extant for Birde's episcopate, 1539-1541). I have therefore with some hesitation omitted Salisbury.
26 Re-admitted.

1930 John David Jones
1931 John Morgan
1934 David Jenkins
1940 John Hughes Jones
1952 John Henry Williams
1965 David Thomas Davies

PREBENDARIES OF PENMYNYDD

1554 William Powell
1584 Henry Roland
1593 Cuthbert Bellot
1613-1616 Held by the bishop
1616 Evan Lloyd
(1617) (1623) Robert White
1660 Robert Morgan
1661 John Gething
1667 Simon Lloyd
1670 Owen Davies
1708 John Williams
1710 Robert Wynn
1720 Owen Hughes
1741 Owen Lloyd
1742 Hugh Hughes
1750 Peter Maurice
1759 Egerton Leigh
1799 Charles Peter Layard
1803 Hugh Wynne Jones
1809 Peter Williams
1818 Henry William Majendie
1870 William Williams
1882 Thomas Williams (Canon Residentiary)
1892 Thomas Warren Trevor
1924 Robert Lloyd Roberts
1930 Henry Lewis James
1933 Henry John Morgan
1934 Thomas John Rowlands
1955 Walis Huw Thomas
1959 John Eric Ramage

TREASURERS

1554 William Roberts
1562 James Ellis
1566 William Bowen[27]
-1613 Griffith Vaughan
1613- Griffith Hughes
(1623) John Lloyd
-1625 Held by the bishop
1625 Rowland Chedle
1660 Michael Evans
1670 Simon Lloyd
1673 John Jones
1689 Owen Eyton
1697 Henry Eyton
1719 Owen Hughes
1720 Peter Maurice
1727 Nicholas Baker
1748 Peter Maurice
1750 Robert Williams
1758 Henry Egerton
1795 Robert Foote
1805 Thomas Ellis
1833 John William Trevor
1860 John Jones
1862 John Owen
1877 Robert Williams
1902 John Fairchild
1943 Gwynfryn Richards
1957 Evan Gilbert Wright
1962 John Humphrey Jones
1966 Hugh Arfon Evans

[27] *C.P.R.* 1563-1566, p. 527. But according to Visitations, Burches and Mason, 1587, Ellis was Treasurer at that date.

CHANCELLORS

(1546) (1561) Thomas Davies
1566 Walter Darell
1570 Richard Byrkedall
1576 William Griffith
1592 Richard Parry
1595 Robert Sherman
1608 Hugh Lewis
1634 Robert Price
1636 William Vaughan
1660 Edward Wynne
1669 Roger Williams
1698 Pierce Lewis
1699 Thomas Vaughan
1705 Hugh Wynne
1720 Evan Jones
1741 Owen Lloyd
1747 Peter Maurice
1748 Thomas Lloyd
1753 John Ellis
1754 Andrew Edwards
1762 Richard Farrington
1772 James Vincent
1783 Lewis Hughes
1816 Henry William Majendie
1818 Hugh Wynne Jones
1849-1851 Vacant
1851 James Williams
1872 Evan Lewis
1887 Thomas Briscoe
1895 Daniel Silvan Evans
1903 John Richards
1908 Owen Lloyd Williams
1919 Cadwgan Powell Price
1931 Francis Parry Watkin Davies
1933 Henry Lewis James
1934 Henry John Morgan
1940 John Williams James
1965 John Henry Williams

PRECENTORS

(1548)-1570 Thomas Bulkeley
1570 John Rowlands
1578 John Price
1582 William Meyrick
1605 Owen Meredith
1613 Arthur Williams
1620 John Baylie
1632 Gabriel Parry
1634 John Griffith[28]
1660 William Lewis
1670 William Brickdall (Birkdale)
1685 Robert Foulkes
1730 Hugh Wynne
1744 Thomas Lloyd
1748 Hugh Hughes
1750 John Ellis
1754 William Lloyd
1796 Thomas Ellis
1805 Hugh Owen
1810 James Henry Cotton
1838-1864 Vacant
1864 Richard Humphrey Hill
1892 Henry Rees
1924 William Williams
1934 Herbert Evans
1943 Evan Jones
1955 Evan Gilbert Wright
1957 Thomas Woodings
1963 David Jonathan Jones
1968 Richard Glyndwr Williams

CANONICUS PRIMUS

-1560 Hugh Vaughan
1560 David Moythey
1583 Hugh Burches
1600 Edmund Griffith
1606 Griffith Hughes
1613 Henry Parry

[28] J. Griffith, canon and prebendary, is attested for 1632 (Visitations).

1617 William Hill
1626 Griffith Pritchard
1633 Hugh Williams
1670 Henry Williams
1703 Thomas Ingram
1712 Nathaniel Humphreys
1725 William Price
1734 Richard Parry
1744 Thomas Jones
1760 Owen Jones
1782 John Williams
1821 Robert Williams
1849-1851 Vacant
1851 William Williams
1868 William Johnson
1892 David Jones
1908 Thomas Edwards
1924 Francis Parry Watkin Davies
1931 David Thomas Jones
1957 Edward Maldwyn Evans

CANONICUS SECUNDUS

-1543 John Trefor
1543 Robert Balfrom
1560 Richard Myrian
1573 David Lloyd
1576 Owen Owens
1581 Robert Morgan
1592 Robert Parry
1600 Henry Moston
1617 Hugh Griffith
1637 Michael Evans
1660 Richard Jeffreys
1667 Lewis Williams
1672 Richard Fletcher
-1679 Robert Wynne
1679 Robert Wynne (another)
1710 John Ellis
1713 Owen Lloyd
1715 David Doulben[29]
1750 James Vincent
1775 John Roberts
1785 Thomas Ellis
1796 Thomas Roberts
1849-1851 Vacant
1851 James Vincent Vincent
1862 Hugh Norris Lloyd
1865 John Arthur Herbert
1875 Daniel Evans
1889 Daniel Silvan Evans
1892 John Morgan
1900 James Rowlands
1901 John Richards
1903 John Lloyd Jones
1907 John Rowlands
1919 Llewelyn Robert Hughes
1925 William Morgan
1934 Richard Hughes Williams
1956 John Humphrey Jones
1962 David Thomas Davies
1965 Evan Orwig Evans

CANONICUS TERTIUS

1554 Thomas Byrkedall (Bryckdale)
1558 Jeffrey Lewis
1560 Maurice Powell
-1592 George Mason
1593 Owen Glyn
1615 William Brunkir
1627 John Annwyl
1634 William Griffiths
(1680) (1696) Robert Roberts

[29] A. I. Pryce doubtfully assigns Doulben's institution to 1715. According to Browne Willis the stall was vacant from 1715 to 1720 or 1721 when Doulben was presented.

c. 1698 Morgan Lewis
1710 Robert Salusbury
1714-1720 Vacant
1720 (or 1721) Richard Nanney
(1723) Bulkeley Hughes
1740 Hugh Hughes
1742 John Owen
1756 Robert Lewis
1766 Richard Griffith
1793 Hugh Owen
1805 John Roberts
1821 Richard Newcombe
1834 Richard Howard
1851-1856 Vacant
1856 Charles Williams
1878 Hon. Francis Godolphin Pelham
1899 John Studholme Brownrigg
1930 Henry John Morgan
1933 John Charles Jones
1941 John Rhys Davies
1953 Harold John Charles
1954 John Richards Richards
1957 William Evans

CANONICUS QUARTUS

1931 Richard Hughes
1947 Gwilym Owen Williams
1949 Henry Williams
1953 Thomas Woodings
1957 Mervyn John Daniel

CANONICUS QUINTUS

1930 Benjamin Jones
1937 John Llewelyn Richards
1943 Alfred Abel
1948 John Eastwood
1955 John Eric Ramage
1960 William Daniel Parry

CANONS RESIDENTIARY

(other than those who combined a residentiary canonry with tenure of one of the old stalls)

1860 John William Trevor
1865 Thomas Thomas
1887 George Griffiths
1889 Eleazar Williams
1891 David Walter Thomas
1903 Edward Hughes
1906 Evan Thomas Davies
1910 Richard Thomas Jones
1917 Edmund Osborne Jones

HONORARY CANONS

1928 Henry Lewis James
1928 Richard Evans
1928 John Lloyd
1932 Lewis Jenkins
1933 William Morgan Morgan Jones
1941 Robert Cybi Jones
1948 Henry Thomas
1949 Morgan Evans Alban
1955 Lemuel Thomas Jones
1965 Hugh Arfon Evans
1966 John Humphreys Jones

CHANTRY PRIESTS AND CONDUCTS

(1504) Richard Wynter (Chantry Priest, St. Catherine's)
(1504) John Norland (Chantry Priest, St. Catherine's)

(1504) Richard Shane (Conduct)
-1518 John Heryng (Chantry Priest, St. Catherine's)
1518-(1535) Thomas ap Goronwy (Chantry Priest, St. Catherine's)[30]
(1535) David Moythey (Chantry Priest)[31]
(1535) Thomas Keynock (Chantry Priest)[32]
(*c.* 1620) Rowland Roberts (Conduct)[33]
(*c.* 1620) Robert Rowlands (Conduct)[33]

VICARS CHORAL

(1504) John Vechan
(1504) Matthew ap Griffith
-1522 Lewis ap Rhys
1522-1534 Hugh Holland
-1536 Richard Mutton (Motton)
1534-1580 Humphrey Birkedale (Brickall)
1536-1542 John Gruff
1542-1572 Rowland Thickens
1572-1573 John Boyes
1573-1578 Robert Morgan
1578-1599 William Sharpe
1580-1607 Robert Williams
1599-1623 John Martyn
1607-1608 Robert Sherman
1608 Roland Mason
1624 Robert Roland
(1623) (1629) William Martin
1641 Thomas Meredith
1660 Thomas Draycot
1661 Owen Evans
1664 Roger Williams
1667 Andrew Matthews
1672 John Buttree
1691 Hugh Johnson
1693 Pierce Lewis
1695 Pierce Lewis[34]
(1699) George Jones
1699 Robert Humphreys
1699 Henry Williams
1708 Henry Williams (another)
1712 Thomas Vincent
1713-1740 Bulkeley Hughes
1714-1744 William Evans
1740-1753 Thomas Lloyd
1744-1750 Hugh Hughes
1750-1785 John Ellis
1753-1760 William Lloyd
1760-1773 James Vincent
1773-1790 Richard Griffith
1785-1810 John Kyffin
1790-1802 Peter Williams
1802-1819 John Jones
1810 John Kyffin (junior)
1810-1838 James Henry Cotton
1819-1858 John Hamer
1838-1850 Hugh Price
1850-1863 Evan Pughe

MINOR CANONS

1858-1866 James Henry Purvis
1859-1862 John Skinner Jones
1863-1874 Charles William Frederick Jones
1866-1872 Lewis Jones
1872-1876 David Henry Ellis
1874-1878 Thomas Rees Walters
1876-1878 Thomas Williams
1878-1886 Owen Evans
1879-1895 Richard Foulkes Jones

[30] *Valor Ecclesiasticus* IV, p. 418.
[31] *ibid.*
[32] *ibid.* VI, p. xvii.
[33] Visitations, Griffiths, 1623.
[34] Apparently a different man from the preceding.

1886-1890 John Thomson Jones
1890-1896 William Morgan Jones
1895-1900 Robert Stephen Edwards
1896-1902 Thomas Edward Owen
1900-1913 Richard Hughes Williams
1902-1903 Thomas Herbert Williams
1903-1907 James Cornelius Morrice
1907-1922 John Eastwood
1913-1920 Maurice Arthur Hughes
1920-1931 Robert Cybi Jones
1922-1923 Rees Jones
1923-1925 Richard Ward
1925-1934 William Davies
1931-1937 John William Evans
1934-1946 Walis Huw Thomas
1938-1942 David Jonathan Jones
1944-1952 Joseph Aelwyn Roberts
1946-1948 Alun Jones
1949-1955 Alexander Gordon McWilliam
1955-1957 Charles Williams Arthur (Succentor)
1958-1960 William Ross Lewis Jones
1958-1962 Edward Thomas Roberts
1963-1965 Brian Arthur Mastin (Chaplain)
1962- Thomas Woodings (Honorary Chaplain)
1967-Francis James Saunders Davies

ORGANISTS

-1644 Thomas Boulton
1691 Thomas Roberts
1705 (Nathaniel?) Priest
1708 — Smith
1710 — Ferrer
1713 John Rathbone
1721 Thomas Rathbone
1750 Thomas Lloyd
1778 Richard Garred (Gerard)
1782 William Shrubsole
1784 Edmund Olive
1793 Joseph Pring
1842 James Sharpe Pring
1868 Robert Roberts
1871 Roland Rogers
1892 Thomas Westlake Morgan
1906 Roland Rogers (re-appointed)
1927 Leslie Douglas Paul

VICARS OF BANGOR

(1391) John Harburgh[35]
(1399) John Walshale[36]
1445-1860 See VICARS CHORAL
1858-1889 Daniel Evans (St. James's from 1866)
1863-1880 John Pryce (St. Mary's from 1864)
1880-1885 John Morgan (St. Mary's)
1886-1913 William Edwards (St. Mary's to 1889, St. James's from 1890)

[35] *C.P.R.* 1391-1396, p. 3.
[36] *ibid.*, 1396-1399, p. 529.

1890-1906 Thomas Edwin Jones (St. Mary's)
1906-1913 William David Roberts (St. Mary's)
1913-1923 John David Jones (St. Mary's 1913; St. James's 1913-1923)
1913-1920 James Cornelius Morrice (St. Mary's)
1920-1935 Lewis Jenkins (St. Mary's)
1923-1937 David Thomas Davies (St. James's)
1935-1937 John Eastwood (St. Mary's)

VICARS OF ST. JAMES'S

1937 David Thomas Davies
1937 John Rhys Davies
1952 Harold John Charles
1954 John Richards Richards
1957 Hywel Islwyn Davies
1962 Edward Thomas Roberts

VICARS OF ST. MARY'S

1937 John Eastwood
1953 Evan John Jones

VICARS OF PENTIR

1888 Herbert Jones
1925 Daniel Thomas
1930 John Roberts
1948 Thomas Glaslyn Williams
1963 Philip Owen Butler

VICARS OF ST. DAVID'S, GLANADDA

1888 Thomas Lewis Jones
1928 William Morgan Morgan-Jones
1931 Robert Cybi Jones
1945 Evan Gilbert Wright
1966 Elwyn Roberts

APPENDIX II

List of Memorials in the Cathedral

NAVE

On west wall, south of tower arch:

1. Nicholas Robinson, Bishop, 1585 (tablet of 1845 replacing original).
2. Henry Rowlands, Bishop, 1616 (see also 9 and 28).
3. Robert Morgan, Bishop, 1673 (see also 12).
4. Margaret, wife of Love Parry, 1684.
5. John Evans, 1699 (see also 15).
6. Thomas Fletcher, 1708.
7. Owen Hughes, Chancellor of the diocese, 1740.

SOUTH AISLE

On nave respond at west:

8. Catherine, wife of William Brynker, 1723.

On south wall:

9. Richard Vaughan, Bishop, 1607, and Henry Rowlands, Bishop, 1616 (originally connected with 28; see also 2).
10. Richard Gwynne, Archdeacon of Bangor, 1617.
11. William Maurice 1668, and Jane his wife, 1649.
12. Robert Morgan, Bishop, 1673, his daughter Catherine, 1682, and granddaughter Anne Humphreys, 1699 (see also 3).
13. Mary Maurice, 1719, and others.
14. John Jones, Dean, 1727.
15. Beata, wife of John Daulben, 1732, and John Evans, 1699 (see also 5).
16. Memorial with modern inscription stating that it was probably of the Williams family of Penrhyn.
17. Pearce Owen Mealy, 1801, and Redway Mealy, 1805.
18. Arthur Rowley Heyland, 1815.
19. James Vincent Vincent, Dean, 1876.
20. James Edmund Vincent, Chancellor of the diocese, 1909.
21. Muriel Gwendolen, wife of Humphrey Owen Jones, 1912.
22. James Trevor Crawley Vincent, 1915.

In floor :

23. Nineteenth-century tablet, not *in situ*, commemorating Owain Gwynedd, 1169.
24. Hugh Hughes, Vicar and Precentor, 1749.
25. Philippa Bethell, 1848.

NORTH AISLE

At west end :

26. Eva, wife of . . . Anwel, fourteenth century.
27. Thomas Williams, 1592, and Jane his wife, 1597 (remains of altar tomb).
28. Headless busts of Richard Vaughan, Bishop, 1607, and Henry Rowlands, Bishop, 1616 (see also 2 and 9).

On north wall :

29. Charles Allanson, 1729.
30. Owen Maurice Owen, 1731, and others.
31. Emily Hamer, 1821, and others.
32. Mary Anne, wife of James Henry Cotton, 1823, and Mary, second wife of James Henry Cotton, 1828.
33. Thomas Ellis, Treasurer, 1833, and others.
34. John Warren, Dean, 1838, and Elizabeth his wife, 1825.
35. Hugh Price, Vicar, 1850, and Penelope his wife, 1866.
36. John Warren, Chancellor of the diocese, 1852.
37. Christopher Bethell, Bishop, 1859.
38. James Henry Cotton, Dean, 1862.
39. William Edward Sackville West, 1905.
40. Bruce Duffus Costen, 1914.
41. John Fitzgerald Prestidge, 1917.
42. Louisa Agnes Griffiths, 1933.

On east wall :

43. Roland Rogers, organist, 1927.

On nave respond at east :

44. Henry William Majendie, Bishop, 1830.
45. Sons of clergy in the diocese killed in wars of 1914-18 and 1939-45.

In floor :

46. John Parry, 1720.
47. Robert Hughes, 1749.
48. Name illegible, eighteenth century.

SOUTH TRANSEPT

On west wall :

49. Goronwy Owen, 1769 (erected 1831).
50. Bangor men killed in war of 1914-18.

In south wall :

51. Slab (early fourteenth century) in tomb recess (late thirteenth century).
52. Edmund Prys, Archdeacon of Merioneth, 1623 (erected on his tercentenary).

On east wall :

53. Henry Thomas Edwards, Dean, 1884.
54. John Charles Jones, Bishop, 1956.

INDEX